Cambridge I

Elements in the Philosophy of Religion
edited by
Yujin Nagasawa
University of Birmingham

COSMOLOGICAL ARGUMENTS

Michael Almeida
University of Texas at San Antonio

CAMBRIDGE
UNIVERSITY PRESS

CAMBRIDGE
UNIVERSITY PRESS

University Printing House, Cambridge CB2 8BS, United Kingdom

One Liberty Plaza, 20th Floor, New York, NY 10006, USA

477 Williamstown Road, Port Melbourne, VIC 3207, Australia

314–321, 3rd Floor, Plot 3, Splendor Forum, Jasola District Centre,
New Delhi – 110025, India

79 Anson Road, #06–04/06, Singapore 079906

Cambridge University Press is part of the University of Cambridge.

It furthers the University's mission by disseminating knowledge in the pursuit of education, learning, and research at the highest international levels of excellence.

www.cambridge.org
Information on this title: www.cambridge.org/ 9781108456920
DOI: 10.1017/9781108675604

© Michael Almeida 2018

First published 2018

A catalogue record for this publication is available from the British Library.

ISBN 978-1-108-45692-0 Paperback
ISSN 2399-5165 (online)
ISSN 2515-9763 (print)

Cosmological Arguments

Michael Almeida

Abstract: *This Element discusses the structure, content, and evaluation of cosmological arguments. The introductory section investigates features essential to cosmological arguments. Traditionally, cosmological arguments are distinguished by their appeal to change, causation, contingency, or objective becoming in the world. But none of these is in fact essential to the formulation of cosmological arguments. Sections 1–3 present a critical discussion of traditional Thomistic, kalām, and Leibnizian cosmological arguments, noting various advantages and disadvantages of these approaches. Section 4 offers an entirely new approach to the cosmological argument – the approach of theistic modal realism. The proper explananda of cosmological arguments on this approach are not change, causation, contingency, or objective becoming in the world. The proper explananda are the totality of metaphysical reality – all actualia and all possibilia. The result is the most compelling and least objectionable version of the cosmological argument.*

Keywords: *cosmological argument, kalām, Aquinas, modal realism, theistic modal realism, actual infinite, modal fatalism, Five Ways, Leibniz, temporal beginning, creation*

ISSNs: 2399-5165 (online), 2515-9763 (print)
ISBNs: 9781108456920 (PB), 9781108675604 (OC)

1 Categorizing Cosmological Arguments

The standard way to categorize cosmological arguments is taxonomically. We begin with a number of theistic arguments that have traditionally been listed under the genus "cosmological." The speciation of cosmological arguments is a function of salient variation in those

traditional arguments. William Lane Craig offers one typology of cosmological arguments based on variation in the role of the infinite
regress.

> During the historical survey of the argument, my attention was drawn
> to one very important feature of the cosmological proof: the role of
> the infinite regress in the argument. ... The first type embraces the
> *kalām* proofs for a beginning of [the] world and the existence of
> a Creator. The second type enfolds all of the proofs in Aquinas's
> first three ways. ... The third type is Leibniz's (and Spinoza's) version
> of the proof. (Craig, 2001: 282ff.)

The Thomistic, kalām, and Leibnizian formulations are undoubt-
edly among the most impressive and powerful species of cosmological arguments. But the taxonomical approach to categorizing
these arguments is largely a matter of practical convenience.
The approach aims to provide some order among an otherwise
disorderly collection of arguments.

The Thomistic, kalām, and Leibnizian cosmological arguments
all offer some *explananda* – whether they are change or motion or
coming to be or contingency – and each argues that the absolute
explanation for these observable features of the universe is an
unmoved mover, a necessary being, an unchanging being, God.
Cosmological arguments do feature essentially some absolute
explanans and some explananda. It's an intriguing metaphysical
question whether cosmological arguments exemplify any other
essential features, or at least whether *successful* cosmological arguments exemplify any other essential features.

The ontological argument is sometimes categorized as the only
a priori argument for the existence of God. William Rowe makes this
the fundamental distinction between cosmological arguments and
ontological arguments.

[Inductive] Arguments for the existence of God are commonly divided into
(Deductive) a [posteriori] arguments and a (priori) arguments. ... Of the three
major arguments for the existence of God – the Cosmological, the
Teleological, and the Ontological – only the last of these is entirely
a priori. In the Cosmological Argument one starts from some simple
fact about the world such as that it contains things which are caused

explaination (...from self-evident propositions)

[relating to or derived from by reasoning from observed facts]

the study of the nature, origin, and limits of human knowledge

to exist by other things. . . . In the Ontological Argument, however, one begins simply with a concept of God. (Rowe, 2007)

Rowe's epistemological basis for distinguishing ontological arguments and cosmological arguments has some historical justification. But must cosmological arguments, or successful cosmological arguments, include a posteriori premises? It is perhaps surprising that facts about change, causation, contingency, and objective becoming that figure so prominently in traditional cosmological arguments are not usefully characterized as a posteriori facts. Cosmological arguments do not necessarily include any a posteriori premises at all. There are indeed cosmological arguments that do not include a single a posteriori premise or assumption.

The proposition that *I am here now* is knowable a priori and so is the proposition that *I exist* (Kaplan, 1979). But surely a cosmological argument could start from simple a priori facts such as I am here now or I exist (Kripke, 1980: 54–56). A cosmological argument might begin with the fact that I am here now and note that this simple a priori fact requires some explanation, as indeed it does. There must be some explanation why I am *here* now and I am not *there* now. There must be some explanation why I exist rather than not exist. The facts that I am here now and that I exist require an explanation because it is a contingent fact that I am here now and a contingent fact that I exist. Some contingent facts that are eligible for explanation are knowable a priori.

Must the explananda of cosmological arguments be the set of contingent facts? Our commitment to *contingent explananda* depends on larger – more or less appealing – ontological commitments. We do observe that objects seem to undergo change and that objects seem to come into existence and go out of existence. G. E. Moore existed in 1920, but he does not exist now. The statue existed yesterday, but does not exist today. Things sure seem to be coming into existence and going out of existence. The cat was sleeping this morning, but the cat is awake now. It was raining yesterday and it is not raining today. Surely something very much like change is occurring.

But it is a mistake to conclude from these observations that it's a contingent fact that it rained or a contingent fact that G. E. Moore existed. It is true that cosmological arguments typically infer from

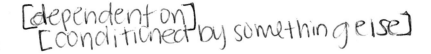

[dependent on]
[conditioned] by something else]

the observation of facts like these that there are contingent explananda. But, strictly speaking, we cannot infer from these observations that there are any contingent explananda at all. In fact, observations like these are neither necessary nor sufficient to establish the existence of contingent explananda.

Benedict de Spinoza famously argued that every object, fact, and event that we observe in the actual world exists, obtains, and occurs as a matter of *extrinsic necessity* (Griffin, 2013). The observation of impermanence in the world – insofar as we actually observe impermanence – does not entail that there are any contingent facts at all.

> Necessitists are not automatically permanentists. .... For a fatalist might be a necessitist by denying all contingency whatsoever, yet still hold that what there is changes on a necessary schedule. (Williamson, 2013: 4)

The observation of objects coming into existence and going out of existence does not entail that any object is contingent (Williamson, 2002, 2013). And the observation that actual objects exemplify a property – say, the color blue – at one time and exemplify another property – say, the color green – at another time does not entail that there are any mutable or changing properties.

In spite of our observations, every property is immutable in Spinozistic worlds. An immutable property is one that an object cannot cease to exemplify and also one that an object cannot begin to exemplify (Morris, 1987).[1] The very same object that we observe to be blue at t and green at t' is, in fact, at all times, essentially blue-at-t and essentially green-at-t'. The very same object that we observe to exist at t and observe not to exist at t' in fact essentially exists-at-t and essentially fails to exist-at-t'.

It is worth noting that our epistemological data not only underdetermine the existence of contingent facts. They also underdetermine the existence of impermanence in the world. We cannot

---

[1] An enduring property is a property that an object exemplifies at some temporal point but could not cease to exemplify at a later temporal point. In addition to enduring properties, there are immemorial properties. These are properties that an object exemplifies and could not have begun, at some temporal point, to exemplify.

determine observationally whether our world is a permanentist world or an impermanentist world. Permanentism is the view that it is always the case that everything is always something (Deasy, 2015). Everything unrestrictedly always exists. According to permanentism, there is no time at which anything comes into, or goes out of, existence. For all our epistemological data can deliver, the world we inhabit is a permanentist Spinozistic world – there is no contingency and objects never come into existence or go out of existence (Linsky and Zalta, 1994; Williamson, 2013). The only explananda for cosmological arguments in permanentist Spinozistic worlds are necessary and permanent objects, events, or facts.

But could necessarily existing, occurring, or obtaining objects, events, or facts be explananda for cosmological arguments? For a contemporary example, we need only consider the many multiverse accounts of creation. The theistic multiverse is a collection of all on-balance good universes and God *necessarily actualizes* the theistic multiverse. Donald Turner offers the following explanation.

> But if a wholly good and omnipotent God exists, then the fact that it would be best if created reality were a certain way does explain why created reality would be that way. The source of selection from among the possible universe ensembles would be the possible universe ensemble that would be the best. *Thus I claim that God ought to actualize that complex possible world which contains cosmoi corresponding to every simple possible world above some cut-off line* – for example, every simple possible world with a favorable balance of good over evil. (Turner, 2003)

The explanandum of cosmological arguments on this account of metaphysical reality is a necessarily existing object – the totality of all on-balance good universes. The explanandum is a necessarily existing object since, according to Turner, God necessarily actualizes the theistic multiverse (Munitz, 1951).[2]

---

[2] Many philosophers have defended various versions of the multiverse. For a historical survey of many-universe hypotheses, see Munitz (1951). Those who take seriously the idea that theism suggests the multiverse include McHarry (1978), Turner (2003), Draper (2004), Hudson (2006), Kraay (2010),

Our observations underdetermine the explananda of cosmological arguments. Our observations are in fact compatible with a wide range of ontological commitments and so a wide range of explananda. It is a consequence of our everyday conceptual scheme that we take ourselves to be observing genuine change, causation, motion, contingency, and objective becoming. And ontological conservatism certainly recommends the deliverances of common sense.

But these everyday ontological commitments are in fact the source of intractable problems for the cosmological argument. These problems range from modal fatalism - sometimes called the problem of *necessitarianism* - to lawless worlds. It is a result of our everyday ontological commitments that the best types of explanation - explanations that really leave nothing unexplained - entail the collapse of all modal distinctions. That is the problem of modal fatalism. It is a result of our everyday commitments that the best explanations entail the impossibility of libertarian freedom and the impossibility of indeterministic quantum effects. It is a result of our commonsense ontology that there are no possible worlds where objects "pop" into existence without causal explanation. But modal imagination informs us that lawless worlds, and many other worlds that are purportedly incompatible with the best explanations, are indeed genuinely possible. Since our naive ontological commitments are the source of such trouble for the cosmological argument, we have at least some reason to reconsider our commitment to commonsense ontology.

Most cosmological arguments assume - implicitly in most cases - that some form of actualist realism is true. That conclusion is a consequence of our commonsense conceptual scheme. Traditional cosmological arguments - Thomistic, Leibnizian, Spinozistic, and kalām - are all committed to some form of actualist realism. The ontological benefits of actualist realism include an intuitive "safe and sane" ontology, ontological economy, and

and O'Connor (2012). For discussion of the difficulties with this view, see Almeida (2008, 2010).

Fatalism: the belief that all events are predetermined

metaphysical conservatism. But the main difficulties with traditional cosmological arguments are in fact traceable to the commonsense commitment to actualist ontologies. It is in fact actualist explananda that generate the problems for absolute explanation, the Bennett–van Inwagen problem of modal fatalism, the problem of modal imagination, the problem of libertarian free will, the problem of lawless worlds, and the problem of indeterministic quantum effects.[3]

There are of course alternative views on the nature of metaphysical reality. Genuine modal realism – more specifically *theistic modal realism* – is a less well-understood, and less well-received, view on the nature of metaphysical reality. According to theistic modal realism, the totality of metaphysical reality is a concrete pluriverse. The concrete pluriverse includes every possible world – all actualia and all possibilia. Possible worlds are spatio-temporally isolated aggregates of world-bound individuals. The explanada of genuine modal realism is far more expansive than the Explanada of actualist realism. The explanada of genuine modal realism includes every possible world and every part of every possible world.

According to theistic modal realism, there is an absolute explanation of the entire pluriverse. Every possible world and everything in every possible world is absolutely explicable. Theistic modal realism does not generate the problems of modal fatalism, modal imagination, libertarian free will, lawless worlds, or indeterministic quantum effects. Theistic modal realism in fact provides us with the most powerful and least objectionable version of the cosmological argument available.

2 Absolute Explanations

Our ontological commitments determine the explananda for which cosmological arguments require an *absolute explanation*.

---

[3] Details about the exact nature of these problems are forthcoming in the sections to follow.

Indeed, it is essential to cosmological arguments to require an absolute explanation.[4] Absolute explanations might better be called genuine total explanations, since absolute explanations are incompatible with the existence of any brute facts. Here is Richard Swinburne.

> Other explanations cite brute facts that form the starting points of explanations; there are no brute facts in absolute explanations – here everything really is explained. (Swinburne, 2004)

There is of course some historical reason to believe that the cosmological argument characteristically depends on some version of the principle of sufficient reason. The principle of sufficient reason is of course an explanatory principle. William Rowe defends such a view.

> It should be clear that no single argument can lay claim to being *the* Cosmological Argument. The Cosmological Argument represents a family of arguments, arguments that generally start from some relatively simple fact about the world and, by appealing to the Principle of Sufficient Reason or some principle governing causality, endeavor to establish the existence of a being that has the properties of the theistic God.
>
> ... Criticisms that may be definitive against one version of the argument may turn out to be utterly irrelevant to some other important version. On the other hand ... all versions of the argument rely on some form of the Principle of Sufficient Reason. (Rowe, 1988)

Rowe assimilates the *principle of causality* to the *principle of sufficient reason* – Leibniz makes the same assimilation – and claims that all versions of the cosmological argument are based on the principle of sufficient reason.

---

[4] This is a controversial claim since philosophers have offered versions of the 'cosmological arguments' with explanatory principles weaker (even much weaker) than absolute explanation. But on these cosmological arguments not everything is explained. We could instead say that it is essential to successful cosmological arguments to require an absolute explanation. On successful cosmological arguments, everything really is explained.

The general principle of causality simply states that, necessarily, for every fact, event, or object there is some causal explanation. It is the denial of the thesis that, possibly, for some existing object there is no causal explanation at all. Some objects rather come into existence *causelessly* and perhaps causelessly *ex nihilo*. The general causal principle requires some causal explanation for each particular fact, event, and object. The principle implausibly entails that there are no possible worlds in which there are no causal laws, and so no causal explanations for the existence, occurrence, or obtaining of anything.

Causal principles do not in general require *absolute explanations*. Causal principles require explanations that terminate in an uncaused cause, or a necessarily existing cause, or an infinite series of causes. Here's a partial analysis of full explanations.

> F is a full explanation of E if F includes both a cause, C, and a reason, R, which together necessitate the occurrence of E'. ... If C and R together provide a full explanation of E, then nothing else logically contingent beside C and R needed to be so in order for the occurrence of E to be guaranteed. (Swinburne, 2004)

A full explanation is one in which the explanans F entails the explanandum E. But F might itself be contingent and unexplained. In a full explanation that is also a "complete explanation," every aspect of the explanandum and explanans at the time of the occurrence is accounted for; nothing explanatorily puzzling remains.

> A complete explanation of the occurrence of E is a full explanation of its occurrence in which all the factors cited are such that there is no [further] explanation (either full or partial) of their existence or operation in terms of factors operative at the time of their existence or operation. (Swinburne, 2004)

So, for example, it might be that high tide is completely explained by the locations of the earth, moon, sun, and water acting in accordance with general relativity. If there is nothing *at the time* of the high tide that explains the locations of the earth, moon, and sun, or the operations of general relativity, then the explanation is complete. Obviously, there is some explanation for the locations of those bodies and the operations of general relativity, but the explanation is some time before the occurrence of high tide.

A complete explanation for an event, state of affairs, or proposition E at t is such that there is no other explanation E' at t for (some or all of) the explanans F of E at t. It is an odd sort of explanation for E. Nonetheless, Alexander Pruss and Richard Swinburne argue that the explanatory principles suitable for the cosmological argument are those that satisfy the conditions of complete explanations.

For Pruss, it is complete explanation that makes possible an acceptable – let's say, a *good enough* – explanation for libertarian free actions.

> My explanatory hypothesis, then, is that x freely chooses A because x is making a free choice between A and B while impressed by the reasons in S.
>
> On my hypothesis, further, had the agent chosen B, the agent would still have been impressed by the reasons in S, but the choice of B would have been explained by x's freely choosing between A and B while impressed by the reasons in T, where T is a set of reasons that favor B over A. Moreover, in the actual world where A is chosen, the agent is also impressed by T. However, in the actual world, the agent does not act on the impressive reasons in T, but on the reasons in S. (Pruss, 2006)

What explains why x does A? The explanation is that x is impressed by the reasons in S for A. What explains why x is actually impressed by S but possibly impressed by T? Nothing does. Reasons S are actually present and known to x, and reasons T are actually present and known to x. x *just happens* to be impressed by the reasons in S. In other words, it's just a brute fact that x is so impressed. That's all there is to say on this form of explanation.

Pruss recognizes that complete explanations are not the best sorts of explanations. But the best sorts of explanations are, in his view, incompatible with libertarian free choice. According to both Pruss and Swinburne, the best sorts of explanations – explanations on which "everything really is explained" – are incompatible with any contingency existing at all.

[L]et us delineate a special kind of ultimate explanation, which I shall call absolute explanation. An absolute explanation of E is an ultimate explanation of E in which the existence and operation of each of the factors cited are either self-explanatory or logically necessary. Other explanations cite brute facts that form the starting points of explanations; there are no brute facts in absolute explanations – here everything really is explained. (Swinburne, 2004: 79ff.)

But Swinburne quickly adds:

I do not believe that there can be any absolute explanations of logically contingent phenomena. . . . You cannot deduce anything logically contingent from anything logically necessary. . . . These are among the many reasons why it must be held that God is a logically contingent being, although maybe one necessary in other ways. (Swinburne, 2004)

Pruss suggests that the best sorts of explanations are not necessary for the cosmological argument.

There is, still, something uncomfortable about the proposed explanation of libertarian action. I think a reader is likely to have the sense that . . . this kind of explanation is explanatorily inferior to, say, deterministic causal explanation or explanation in terms of a necessitating metaphysical principle. That may be. But there is no need to take the PSR to say that there is always the best kind of explanation – the PSR I am defending merely says that there is an explanation of every contingent proposition. And that is all I need for the cosmological argument. (Pruss, 2009b)

Swinburne shares this view about the implications of absolute explanation for free action – the freedom of God, in this case. He too thinks that cosmological arguments can get by with less than the best explanations.

[L]et us leave aside consideration of absolute explanation, and return to explanations of other types. I suggest that the arguments to the existence of God . . . are arguments to a complete explanation of the phenomena. They all claim that God's widest intention at some time brings about certain phenomena at that time; and that nothing else at that time explains either his existence or his forming that intention. His intention involved in a complete explanation has no causal explanation at all, since he is perfectly free. (Swinburne, 2004: 80)

Swinburne and Pruss both argue that the theoretical costs of absolute explanations outweigh the benefits of having the best type of explanation. The theoretical costs of the best explanations include abandoning libertarian free will and abandoning all contingency. But they also include the irresolvable problems of modal fatalism, modal imagination, and indeterministic quantum effects. These costs are far greater than the benefits of absolute explanations. Swinburne and Pruss of course acknowledge that absolute explanations are the best kinds of explanation. Absolute explanations genuinely explain everything. But the costs of the best explanations are too great.[5]

But Pruss and Swinburne are mistaken in attributing serious theoretical costs to absolute explanations. As we observed earlier, the theoretical costs cited are all due to the ontological commitments in actualist realism. It is a consequence of actualist realism that the explananda of cosmological arguments are concrete states of affairs or true propositions or actually occurring events or actually existing objects. It is a consequence of the ontological commitment to an absolutely actual world that the explananda of cosmological arguments include only absolute actualia. These commitments generate the problems of libertarian free will, modal fatalism, modal imagination, and indeterministic quantum effects. The commitments also generate the necessity of – at least as Swinburne sees it – a *contingent God.*

---

[5] Absolute explanations exemplify the virtues of completeness and ultimacy. Completeness ensures that everything is explained (there are no brute facts) and ultimacy ensures that explanation terminates in a self-explained unmoved mover, necessary being, unchanging being, God.

3   Are Cosmological Arguments Essentially Invalid?

It would be fascinating to discover that cosmological arguments are essentially invalid. But could it be shown that no cosmological argument *could have* a valid form? According to Richard Swinburne, a proof exists that there cannot be a valid, deductive cosmological argument. Here is Swinburne.

> The starting points of cosmological arguments are evident facets of experience. There is no doubt about the truth of statements that report that they hold. It seems to me equally evident that no argument from any such starting points to the existence of God is deductively valid. (Swinburne, 2004: 136)

But what are the evident facets of experience that Swinburne has in mind? What facets of experience are such that it is not possible to move validly from statements about those facets to the conclusion that God exists?

> Kant defined a cosmological argument as one that starts from "experience that is purely indeterminate" or "experience of existence in general." Let us say, more precisely, that it is one that starts from the existence of a finite object – that is an object of limited power, knowledge, or freedom – that is, any object other than God. However, other arguments called cosmological have in effect started from something rather more specific, the existence of a complex physical universe; and I shall confine my discussion mainly to these. (Swinburne, 2004: 133)

According to Swinburne, it is evident that we cannot validly conclude from the totality of the physical universe that God exists.

> For, if an argument from, for example, the existence of a complex physical universe to the existence of God were valid, then it would be incoherent to assert that a complex physical universe exists and that God does not exist. There would be a hidden contradiction buried in such co-assertions. Now, the only way to prove a proposition to be incoherent is to deduce from it an *obviously* incoherent proposition (for example, a self-contradictory proposition), but, notoriously,

attempts to derive obviously incoherent propositions from such co-
assertions have failed through commission of some elementary logical error. (Swinburne, 2004: 136)

Swinburne concludes that we should instead advance inductive
cosmological arguments that either increase the probability that
God caused the universe or make it more probable than not that
God caused the universe.[6]

But let's consider Swinburne's criterion that if there were a valid
inference from the existence of a complex physical universe to the
existence of God, then it would be incoherent to assert that
a complex physical universe exists and that God does not exist.
This is a peculiar criterion to advance, since there are always
straightforwardly valid inferences from any proposition p to any
other proposition q.

(I)
(1) $p \rightarrow q$
(2) p
(3) $\therefore q$

The argument form in (I) from p to q is obviously valid. Does it
follow that, for any propositions p and q, the proposition p & ~q is
incoherent? That's hardly credible.

Perhaps what Swinburne is worried about are valid cosmological
arguments from the existence of the universe to the existence of
God whose auxiliary premises are all necessary. Cosmological
arguments on this view would assert – in addition to being valid –
that there are no possible worlds in which there is a physical
universe and God does not exist. Consider the valid argument
form in (II).

(II)
(1') $\Box(p \rightarrow q)$
(2') p
(3') $\therefore q$

---

[6] See Reichenbach (2017).

The argument from the physical universe to the necessary existence of God is a substitution instance of this argument form. And
of course all of the auxiliary premises – namely, premise (1) – are
necessary. But we have the same problem we had earlier. For any
two propositions p and q we can construct a substitution instance
of the valid form in (II). But, of course, it is false that any two
propositions are incoherent.

The syntactic criterion that Swinburne offers for demonstrating
that propositions are incoherent cannot be correct. An adequate
criterion of coherence would have to be a semantic criterion. If an
argument from the existence of a complex physical universe to the
existence of God were *sound*, then it would be incoherent to assert
that a complex physical universe exists and that God does not
exist.

Let's take Swinburne as aiming to show that there are no
sound cosmological arguments from the physical universe to
the existence of God. So how do we prove that the proposition
that a complex physical universe exists and God does not exist
is coherent? The proof must show that there is some coherent
proposition r that entails the conjunction that a physical universe exists and God does not exist. The structure of the argu-
ment is that if $\Box(r \rightarrow (p \text{ \& } q))$ and $\Diamond r$, then $\Diamond(p \text{ \& } q)$. Here is
Swinburne.

> So to prove one statement coherent you need to assume that some
> other statement (or conjunction of statements) is coherent. You can
> prove p to be coherent if you can show that it follows deductively
> from another statement r which is coherent. For if r makes
> a coherent statement about the world and p follows deductively
> from r ... p must also be coherent. (Swinburne, 1993: 39)

Coherent propositions are just consistent propositions, or propositions that do not entail a contradiction. Note that this is
just the method that Alvin Plantinga uses to prove that the
proposition that God is omnipotent, omniscient, and wholly
good is consistent with the proposition that there is evil in
the world.

Now one way to show that a proposition p is consistent with a proposition q is to produce a third proposition r whose conjunction with p is consistent and entails q. r, of course, need not be true or known to be true; it need not be so much as plausible. All that is needed is for it to be consistent with p, and in conjunction with the latter, entail q. (Plantinga, 1974b: 165)

Plantinga uses the formula $\Box((r \& p) \rightarrow q)$, and the structure of his argument is $\Box((r \& p) \rightarrow q))$ and $\Diamond(r \& p)$, then $\Diamond(p \& q)$.

For Plantinga, the proposition that plays the role of r is that God has good reasons to permit some instances of evil. But what plays the role of r for Swinburne?

[I]t seems easy enough to spell out in an obviously coherent way a way in which such co-assertion would be true. There would be a complex universe and no God, if there had always been matter rearranging itself in various combinations, and the only persons had been embodied persons; if there was never a person who knew everything, or could do everything, etc. Atheism does seem to be a supposition consistent with the existence of a complex physical universe, such as our universe. Of course, things may not be as they seem, but, in the absence of any worthwhile argument to the contrary known to me, I shall assume that the non-existence of God is logically compatible with the existence of the universe, and so that the cosmological argument is not valid, and so not a good deductive argument. (Swinburne, 2004: 136–137)

The proposition that plays the role of r appears to be *there had always been matter rearranging itself in various combinations, and the only persons had been embodied persons; if there was never a person who knew everything, or could do everything.* Swinburne's proposition r does entail that a complex universe exists and God does not exist, but the argument from r is just question begging. After all, what is to be shown is that, possibly, there is a complex physical universe and there never was a person who knew everything or could do everything. But that is just proposition r. Setting aside the issue of locating some proposition to play the role of r, the main problem is Swinburne's criterion of obvious coherence or obvious consistency.

Many inconsistent sets of propositions entail contradictions only on the assumption of additional logical and metaphysical truths. J. L. Mackie famously argued that it is inconsistent that both God exists and there is evil. But the inconsistency is not formal and not explicit.

> However, the contradiction does not arise immediately; to show it we need some additional premises, or perhaps some quasi-logical rules connecting the terms "good," and "evil" and "omnipotent." These additional principles are that good is opposed to evil, in such a way that a good thing always eliminates evil as far as it can, and that there are no limits to what an omnipotent thing can do. From these it follows that a good omnipotent thing eliminates evil completely, and then the proposition that a good omnipotent thing exists, and that evil exists, are incompatible. (Mackie, 1955: 201)

The set S = {God exists, Evil exists} is not explicitly inconsistent. There is no explicit contradiction in S. But the set is also not formally inconsistent. There are no axioms or inference rules that we might apply to the propositions in S to derive a contradiction. Since S follows from the coherent proposition that a being exists exemplifying the divine attributes in the actual world and the actual world includes instances of evil, S satisfies Swinburne's criterion of obvious consistency. But, despite the obvious consistency, Mackie argues convincingly that set S includes an implicit contradiction. There are metaphysical principles – viz., a good thing always eliminates evil as far as it can and there are no limits to what an omnipotent thing can do – whose addition to S makes S formally inconsistent.

Similarly, of course, the set S' = {there exists a complex physical universe, God does not exist} is neither explicitly nor formally inconsistent. But S' is implicitly inconsistent. There are metaphysical principles – viz., there is an absolute explanation for any complex physical universe and no complex physical universe is self-explanatory – whose addition to S makes S formally inconsistent.

The metaphysical principle that there is an absolute explanation for any complex physical universe requires that universes have the best types of explanations. Some philosophers – Swinburne, Pruss, and van Inwagen included – reject the thesis that our universe has the best type of explanation. But the reasons for rejecting that explanatory thesis are bad ones. Swinburne and others reject the explanatory thesis because of a mistaken commitment to actualist realism. As we noted earlier, the metaphysical thesis that should be abandoned is actualist realism, since it is the source of so many problems for the cosmological argument.

4 Plan of the Element

In Section 1, there is a review and evaluation of three Thomistic cosmological arguments. These are the first three arguments in Aquinas's famous five ways. The argument from change or motion – Aquinas's first way – raises fascinating questions about the nature of causation, the possibility of self-causation, and the possibility of infinite causal chains. The second way, the argument from efficient causation, is based on the observation of objects coming into existence and going out of existence and aims to show that there must be an uncaused cause. The argument raises questions about the nature of causal efficacy and the possibility of efficacious infinite chains.

The third way is the argument from contingency and it is based on the observation of corruptible objects. These are objects that are able to exist and able not to exist. The argument for a necessary being in the third way has received a lot of criticism. Aquinas (in)famously asserts in that argument that if everything were contingent, then there would be a time at which nothing existed. Aquinas might cogently argue instead that if every object were contingent, then there would have been a time at which every object came into existence self-caused. And that conclusion is at least as unacceptable as the conclusion that there would have been a time at which there were no objects, and it serves the argument at least as well. The third way, I suggest, is much more powerful than commonly believed.

In Section 2, the kalām cosmological argument is presented and evaluated. The kalām cosmological argument's most prominent contemporary expositor and defender is William Lane Craig, and a vast literature on the argument has emerged. Craig's a priori argument for a beginning to the universe aims to establish the Aristotelian thesis that an "actual infinite" is impossible. There could not be an infinite temporal regress of events – or, as Craig often puts it, there could not be an infinite series in the "real world" – therefore, the universe had some temporal beginning. It is argued in Section 2 that none of the arguments against an actual infinite is conclusive.

Section 3 focuses attention on Leibnizian cosmological arguments. The explanatory principle in Leibnizian arguments is the principle of sufficient reason. The discussion in Section 3 considers the major objections to Leibnizian cosmological arguments, including the Hume–Edwards objection to world-explanations and the objections from modal fatalism, contingency, libertarian freedom, modal imagination, and indeterministic quantum effects.

It is argued in Section 4 that theistic modal realism offers the most powerful version of the cosmological argument. The relevant explanandum is a vast metaphysical reality – every possible world and every part of every possible world. The cosmological argument concludes that God necessarily creates the totality of metaphysical reality, so it is certainly true that no part of the pluriverse could have been any different. Nonetheless there is contingency in the pluriverse. Contingency arises in complex ways from variation in the standards of similarity that determine counterpart relations. Further, there are straightforward ways in which causally indeterministic, libertarian free, causally lawless, and other modally imaginable worlds are all accommodated in the concrete pluriverse.

Section 1   Thomistic Cosmological Arguments

For when someone wants to support faith by unconvincing arguments, he becomes a laughing stock for the unbelievers, who think that we rely on such arguments and believe because of them.

(Aquinas, 2008: 1a. 32. 1)

St. Thomas Aquinas believed that his five arguments were not probabilistic arguments but rather five distinct demonstrations of the existence of God. Of the five ways, only the first three are properly categorized as cosmological arguments. The arguments proceed from three distinct observations – observations of change, causation, and contingency in the world – to the existence of some ultimate Being that is the cause of these in the world.

Each of the three cosmological ways is typically categorized as an a posteriori argument. Part of the reason that the cosmological arguments are a posteriori is that, according to Aquinas's empiricist epistemology, there are no cogent a priori arguments for the existence of God. Indeed, Aquinas offers a "refutation" of a priori proofs for God's existence in the *Summa* (Aquinas, 2008: 1a. 2. 1). Concerning the existence of a being than which none greater can be conceived Aquinas notes:

> [G]ranted that everyone understands that by this word "God" is signified something than which nothing greater can be thought, nevertheless, it does not therefore follow that he understands that what the word signifies exists actually, but only that it exists mentally. Nor can it be argued that it actually exists, unless it be admitted that there actually exists something than which nothing greater can be thought; and this precisely is not admitted by those who hold that God does not exist. (Aquinas, 2008: 1a. 2. 1)

The only way to prove that God exists is through the effects of God in the world. William Lane Craig concurs with the traditional categorization of the three cosmological arguments as a posteriori proofs.

> [E]ach proof itself is clearly a posteriori. As Aquinas looks out at the world, he sees that some things are changing, some things are being caused, and some things are coming into being and passing away. Each proof begins with some aspect of empirical reality and reasons to a transcendent ground for that aspect of reality. The first three ways then are all a posteriori. (Craig, 2001: 160)

But what is the significance of categorizing them as a posteriori? As we've noted, all of these a posteriori propositions might be necessarily true. The fact that there is change in the world, things being caused, and things coming into existence and going out of existence is consistent with every event, fact, object, and proposition being necessary. We need to keep in mind that no observational fact is inconsistent with our world being a Spinozistic world or, for that matter, a multiverse world in which everything occurs necessarily, exists necessarily, or obtains necessarily.[7] But it does seem crucial to Aquinas's arguments that these facts, objects, events, and propositions are not themselves necessary, whether or not they are a posteriori.

1.1 Aquinas's First Way

Aquinas presents the following version of the argument for God's existence from change or motion in the *Summa Theologica*. According to Aquinas, it is the most obvious way.

> The first and clearest way is that taken from movement or change (ex parte motus): It is certain, and obvious to the senses, that in this world some things are moved. But everything that is moved is moved by another. For nothing is moved except insofar as it is in potentiality with respect to that actuality toward which it is moved, whereas something effects movement insofar as it is in actuality in a relevant respect. After all, to effect movement (movere) is just to lead something from potentiality into actuality. But a thing cannot be led from potentiality into actuality except through some being that is in actuality in a relevant respect; for example, something that is hot in actuality – say, a fire – makes a piece of wood, which is hot in potentiality, to be hot in actuality, and it thereby moves and alters the piece of wood. But it is impossible for something to be simultaneously in potentiality and in actuality with respect to same thing; rather, it can be in potentiality and in actuality only with respect to different things. For what is hot in actuality cannot simultaneously

---

[7] See, for instance, Kraay (2011), Turner (2003, 2014).

be hot in potentiality; rather, it is cold in potentiality. Therefore, it is impossible that something should be both mover and moved in the same way and with respect to the same thing, or, in other words, that something should move itself. Therefore, everything that is moved must be moved by another. If, then, that by which something is moved is itself moved, then it, too, must be moved by another, and that other by still another. But this does not go on to infinity. For if it did, then there would not be any first mover and, as a result, none of the others would effect movement, either. For secondary movers effect movement only because they are being moved by a first mover, just as a stick does not effect movement except because it is being moved by a hand. Therefore, one has to arrive at some first mover that is not being moved by anything. And this is what everyone takes to be a God. (Aquinas, 2008: 1a. 2. 3)

The first premise in Aquinas's first way – his argument for the unmoved mover – observes that change is occurring. The premise is that it is obvious to the senses that some things in the world are in the process of change or movement. The sort of change Aquinas had in mind is change in quantity, quality, or place. And indeed it is obvious to the senses that some things are in the process of changing in each of these ways.

The second premise in the proof is that anything in the process of change is being changed by something else. An object that changes from blue to green is, in Aquinas's terms, potentially green and actually blue. The process of change is the process of moving from being potentially blue to being actually blue.

But could anything simply cause itself to change from blue to green? Could anything that is blue cause itself to become green? Aquinas denies that anything could cause itself to actualize some potentiality. But what is the argument?

But a thing cannot be led from potentiality into actuality except through some being that is in actuality in a relevant respect; for example, something that is hot in actuality – say, a fire – makes a piece of wood, which is hot in potentiality, to be hot in actuality, and it thereby moves and alters the piece of wood. But it is impossible for something to be simultaneously in potentiality and in actuality with respect to the same thing; rather, it can be in potentiality and in actuality only with respect to different things.

For what is hot in actuality cannot simultaneously be hot in potentiality; rather, it is cold in potentiality. Therefore, it is impossible that something should be both mover and moved in the same way and with respect to the same thing, or, in other words, that something should move itself. Therefore, everything that is moved must be moved by another. (Aquinas, 2008: 1a. 2. 3)

The argument here appears to be the following. If y is actually F and potentially G, and x is the cause of y actualizing G, then x must be G. So, if y is the cause of y actualizing G, then y must already be G. Therefore, if y is the cause of y actualizing G, then y is both actually G and potentially G, and that is impossible. Therefore nothing causes itself to move or undergo change.

Aquinas's argument against self-causation is unfortunate. It entails that anything x that causes y to be some property G must itself be G. Thus, taken at his literal word, the fire that causes the wood to be hot must itself be hot. But it is obvious that something might cause an object to become green without actually being green. Copper undergoes chemical reactions that cause the metal to change to a pale green. But the cause is not pale green. Similarly corroding iron changes from silver to orange-red. The cause of this change is not itself orange-red. Examples are easy to multiply.

According to William Lane Craig, the bad news is that the argument that Aquinas offers here is not good. The good news is that it is not central to his main argument.

His example of fire and wood, introduced at this point, is bound to be misleading and is irrelevant to the main line of argument. . . . By producing counterexamples, which is very easy, they believe that they have dealt the argument a fatal blow. But this is to treat Aquinas's proof in an unsympathetic manner. The real thrust of the proof is that the actualizing of a potential can only be done by an actual thing. (Craig, 2001: 173)

It is worth noting that Craig is probably mistaken about the main thrust of the proof at this point. What Aquinas is arguing here is that nothing can cause itself to change, and the argument for that conclusion relies on the assumption that the cause of change must actually have the property it is causing another object to actualize. If Aquinas were arguing for the conclusion that only an actual thing can cause another thing to actualize some property, then there would be no reason to believe that an actual blue thing cannot cause itself to actualize the property of being green. The blue thing is an actual thing, after all. But such self-causation is precisely what Aquinas is anxious to deny.

It is perhaps best to argue that the concept of a genuinely self-causing object is incoherent. All of the examples of alleged self-causation fail to be instances of genuine self-causation. There are no instances in which an object x causes the very same object x to actualize or instantiate some property P.[8] Rather we find examples of one stage or temporal part of an object—allowing ourselves to speak of temporal parts for the moment – standing in some causal relation to another stage or temporal part of that same object. An earlier stage of you, for instance, might cause the current stage of you to do well on an exam today. But this is no interesting form of self-causation. It is reasonable to suppose, then, that anything in the process of change is being changed by something else.

The third premise in the argument is just a generalization of premise two. For any object x, if x is undergoing change, then the change in x is being caused by some object y where $x \neq y$. The generalization rules out self-caused change, of course, but it also rules out uncaused change. It is an endorsement of a principle of causation requiring that there be no effects – broadly speaking, occurrences, facts, states of affairs, objects, changes – without causes.

Aquinas's conception of causation is not the contemporary view that causation is a relation (typically counterfactual) between events. Causation is rather a broad relation of ontological

---

[8] Arguments for the self-causation of the universe are not arguments for genuine self-causation. See, for instance, Smith (2008).

dependence between things (Cohoe, 2013). According to Aquinas, it is part of the very idea of cause and effect that effects depend ontologically on their causes. The causes Aquinas acknowledges are the four Aristotelian causes – efficient, final, formal, and material – and he argues that in each case effects depend ontologically on their causes.[9] Composite objects cease to exist, of course, in the absence of their material parts or formal causes. These are ontological constituents of composite objects. But in the absence of their efficient or final causes, effects would also cease to exist. There are, then, no uncaused effects, just as the principle of causation requires.[10]

The principle of causation is perhaps no more complicated than we find in the following formulation.

> Thomistic arguments posit an intuitively plausible Causal Principle (CP) that says that every item of some sort, e.g., event, contingent being, instance of coming-into-existence, or movement, has a cause. . . . The Thomistic argument, exemplified by Aquinas' first three ways, does not rule out the possibility of an infinite past, but uses a variety of methods to argue against the hypothesis that there is an infinite regress of causes with no first cause. (Pruss, 2009)

The principle of causation is plausible, especially when properly qualified to include both causes per se, or non-incidental causes, and causes per accidens, or incidental causes. Causes per accidens provide a way to introduce non-necessitating causes or, we might say, probabilistic causes – the meteorite striking at this particular location at this particular time, or the earthquake occurring at the exact location and time that it does occur. For Aquinas, these have causes too, but they do not have necessitating causes.

The fourth premise in the first way is certainly the most interesting and controversial premise in the argument. Aquinas's fourth premise states that if that by which something is moved is itself

---

[9] There are in addition Platonic ideal causes in Aquinas that exist in the mind of God.

[10] According to Aquinas, there are effects that do not have necessitating causes, but rather have per accidens causes. See Aquinas (2008: 1a 115.6).

moved, then it too must be moved by another, and that other by still another. But this does not go on to infinity. The series of causes is not endless or infinite; indeed, it cannot be, according to Aquinas. He offers the following argument.

> But this does not go on to infinity. For if it did, then there would not be any first mover and, as a result, none of the others would effect movement, either. For secondary movers effect movement only because they are being moved by a first mover, just as a stick does not effect movement except because it is being moved by a hand. Therefore, one has to arrive at some first mover that is not being moved by anything. And this is what everyone takes to be a God. (Aquinas, 2008: 1a. 2. 3)

Secondary or intermediate movers have no causal efficacy in the absence of a primary mover. The metaphysical question is not whether Aquinas understands secondary or intermediate movers correctly – he can simply stipulate that this is what he means by "intermediate mover." The metaphysical question is whether what we observe in the world are intermediate causes in Aquinas's sense of the term. Keeping in mind that causation is a relation of onto-logical dependence for Aquinas, the motion of the intermediate causes is ontologically dependent on the motion of some non-intermediate cause. Intermediate causes have all causal efficacy derivatively and not merely from some temporally or ontologically proximate cause. There are no proximate or nearest causes except the entire causal series antecedent to the motion of some object. The series cannot include only intermediate or derivative causes since no derivative cause can derive its causal efficacy from deri-vative causes alone. To borrow Aquinas's metaphor, there is no world in which the stick derives its motion from the motion of another stick and that from the motion of another and so on infinitely in a series of derivative causes, since such a series would entail that derived causes can derive their causal efficacy exclusively from derived causes. According to Aquinas, that is not possible. But do examples exist of this sort of ontological dependence?

> To give an illustration of the sort of dependence on prior members which Aquinas has in mind, consider a flower pot suspended by a chain of rings. The bottom ring holds up the flowerpot, but it holds up the flowerpot only in virtue of being held up by the ring above it which, in turn, holds up the ring and the flower pot only because it is held up by the ring above it. Each ring is a held-up holder up, if you will. In such a series, each ring is simultaneously active in holding up the posterior rings and passive in being held up by the prior rings and whatever holds them up. (Cohoe, 2013)

Of course the image is one in which an infinite series of rings would have no more efficacy in holding up the flowerpot than a finite series of rings. In either case we need some independent source of causal efficacy that confers efficacy on all of the dependent rings. Since the flowerpot is indeed held up, there must be an ultimate source of causal efficacy.

The suggestion that an infinite series of causally dependent objects or events might provide sufficient explanation for the motion we observe misunderstands the notion of an ordered series or essentially ordered series. The causal relation in these series is transitive, asymmetric, and irreflexive. But more importantly the causal relation is *hyper-derivative*. Consider the finite causal series S, e $\longrightarrow$ e' where the arrow represents the causal relation. If e and e' are derivative causes, the problem with the series S is not merely that e has no cause. The problem is that neither e nor e' has a cause. No derivative cause is causally efficacious on its own, so e is not a cause of e'. There is, in effect, no causation at all in the series S.

Let's imagine, then, a world w in which e simply occurs and causes e'. Such a world is not a possible world, according to Aquinas, since e's occurrence in w has no causal explanation. Since e is an intermediate or derivative cause, w is a world in which e derives its causal efficacy from nothing at all. But what about the occurrence of e' in w? It is also true that the occurrence of e' is not possible. It is not possible that e' is caused by an intermediate cause that did not derive its efficacy from a source that *could be* the source of such efficacy. The only source of causal efficacy is a nonderivative cause.

But then consider the series S', e $\longrightarrow$ e' $\longrightarrow$ e" where e' and e" are derivative causes and e is a nonderivative cause. In series S', e' is again not a cause of e", since no derivative cause is efficacious on its own. In S' either the two elements in the series (e & e') cause e" or e causes e" via the intermediate cause e'. In either case, there is no causal efficacy in the intermediate causes unless there is nonderivative cause in the series. Finally, in the infinite series S_ω, $e_\omega \longrightarrow e_{\omega-1}$ $\longrightarrow \ldots \longrightarrow e_n \longrightarrow e_{n-1} \longrightarrow \ldots \longrightarrow e_1 \longrightarrow e_0$ the cause of e_0 would have to include some nonderivative cause e_n in S_ω. But no matter which e_n in the series we select as a nonderivative cause of e_0, n is some finite number. The cause of e_0 terminates in some nonderivative cause e_n in a finite series. If the causal series in S contained nonderivative causes then the series might be infinitely long, since it might be the case that $(e_\omega \longrightarrow e_{\omega-1}) \longrightarrow \ldots \longrightarrow (e_n \longrightarrow e_{n-1}) \longrightarrow \ldots \longrightarrow (e_1 \longrightarrow e_0)$, where the nonderivative causes are e_1, e_3, e_5, and so on. For an example, we can imagine an occasionalist model wherein God causes e_0, e_2, e_4, and so on infinitely, or a set of accidental causes going back infinitely.

1.2 Aquinas's Second Way

The argument against an infinite series of derivative causes in what Aquinas calls an ordered series is a reductio ad absurdum. The argument is essentially the same in the first three ways. In the second way – the argument from efficient causation – Aquinas argues for a finitude of causes as follows.

> But it is impossible to go on to infinity among efficient causes. For in every case of ordered efficient causes, the first is a cause of the intermediate and the intermediate is a cause of the last – and this regardless of whether the intermediate is constituted by many causes or by just one. But when a cause is removed, its effect is removed. Therefore, if there were no first among the efficient causes, then neither would there be a last or an intermediate. But if the efficient causes went on to infinity, there would not be a first efficient cause, and so there would not be a last effect or any intermediate efficient causes, either – which is obviously false.

Therefore, one must posit some first efficient cause – which everyone calls a God. (Aquinas, 2008: 1a. 2. 3)

The argument from efficient causation is not, of course, an argument from motion or change, but an argument from existence.
The observation is that we observe some objects causing other
objects to come into existence and go out of existence.
The argument in the second way is an argument from the existence
of things to the existence of an uncaused cause. There cannot be an
infinitude of intermediate or dependent causes, according to
Aquinas, for the same reason there cannot be an infinitude of
mover movers. The causal efficacy of intermediate efficient causes
depends on an independent source of efficacy. If there were no
such independent source of causal efficacy, then there would be no
efficient causation occurring, contrary to our observations.

1.3 Aquinas's Third Way

In the third way – the argument from contingency – Aquinas observes
that there are corruptible objects and argues that not every object can
be corruptible. Not every object can be the sort of object that is able to
exist and able not to exist, or not every being is contingent.

> But it is impossible that everything that exists should be like this;
> for that which is able not to exist is such that at some time it
> does not exist. Therefore, if everything is such that it is able not
> to exist, then at some time nothing existed in the world. But if
> this were true, then nothing would exist even now. For what does
> not exist begins to exist only through something that does exist;
> therefore, if there were no beings, then it was impossible that
> anything should have begun to exist, and so nothing would exist
> now – which is obviously false. Therefore, not all beings are able
> to exist [and able not to exist]; rather, it must be that there is
> something necessary in the world. (Aquinas, 2008: 1a. 2. 3)

The observation that there are contingent beings seems innocuous
and it is generally accepted as such. But it is important to note that

there really is no observation that informs us that an object, event, state of affairs, or whatnot is contingent. The fact that objects are corruptible, for instance, does not, strictly speaking, inform us that those objects are contingent, since corruptible objects might nonetheless exist necessarily.

On Thomistic metaphysics, though, contingent beings are understood temporally. Contingent beings are those that come into existence at some time and go out of existence at some time.

> Certain of the things we find in the world are able to exist and able not
> to exist (quaedam quae sunt possibilia esse et non esse); for some
> things are found to be generated and corrupted and, as a result, they
> are able to exist and able not to exist. (Aquinas, 2008: 1a. 2. 3)

And surely we can observe that there are such objects, whether or not they, in contemporary terms, necessarily exist.

The most controversial premise in the third way states that "it is impossible that everything should be like this." It is impossible that everything should be a contingent object. It is impossible, according to Aquinas, because if everything were contingent, then there would have been a time at which nothing existed. And if there had been a time at which nothing existed, then nothing would exist now. This particular argument in the third way can seem fallacious, and Aquinas does not offer a cogent argument for either conclusion in the *Summa*. Superficially the argument appears to commit the quantifier-shift fallacy. It seems to go from a premise of the form *for every x, there is some time t such that Fx at t*, to a conclusion of the form *there is some time t such that, for every x, Fx at t* or briefly from $(\forall x)(\exists y)Fxy$ to $(\exists y)(\forall x)Fxy$. That argument form is invalid in first-order logic.

It is not clear that there is a valid argument for the conclusion that there was a time at which no contingent objects existed. But there is a valid argument for the conclusion that there was a time at which contingent objects came into existence self-caused. Aquinas can cogently argue that if every object were contingent, then there would have been a time at which every object came into existence self-caused. Suppose every object were a contingent object. If so,

then there was a time at which contingent objects caused themselves to exist. How so? There are really only two cases to consider.
In case (i), the past is temporally finite and there is a beginning to
the universe. Suppose the universe began at time t. If so, then the
first contingent objects came into existence at some time $t \geq 0$.
It might have been the case that for all times t onward there existed
contingent objects, so there was no time at which there were no
contingent objects. Nonetheless the objects that exist at t must
have come into existence self-caused, since there exist contingent
objects and there are no contingent objects prior to t.

In case (ii), the past is infinite and there is no beginning to the
universe. Suppose the past is infinite and there is some nonzero
probability p that no contingent objects exist at all. If there is some
positive probability p that no contingent objects exist and the past
is in fact infinite, then it was the case, sometime in the past, that
there are no contingent objects. Over an infinite span of time every
state of affairs that has some positive probability of occurring does
occur. In case (ii) again there is some time t in the past at which
contingent objects came into existence self-caused, since it was the
case that no contingent objects existed at all.

The hypothesis that every object is a contingent object entails that
there is some time t at which contingent objects caused themselves
to come into existence. Since Aquinas takes the reasonable position
that no contingent object can cause itself to exist, it follows that the
hypothesis is mistaken. It is false that every object is a contingent
object. Therefore there must exist some necessary objects.

It is an important distinction that, according to Aquinas, some
necessary objects have their necessity "caused from outside" of
themselves and some necessary objects do not have their necessity
caused at all. He offers a reductio ad absurdum, exactly analogous
to those given earlier, that not every necessary being can have its
necessity caused.

> Now every necessary being either has a cause of its necessity from
> outside itself or it does not. But it is impossible to go on to infinity
> among necessary beings that have a cause of their necessity – in the

same way, as was proved above, that it is impossible to go on to infinity among efficient causes. Therefore, one must posit something that is necessary per se, which does not have a cause of its necessity from outside itself but is instead a cause of necessity for the other necessary things. But this everyone calls a God. (Aquinas, 2008: 1a. 2. 3)

There cannot be an infinitude of intermediate causes in this case for the same reason that there cannot be an infinitude of moved movers. The efficacy of intermediate causes in causing necessity depends on an independent source of necessity. If there were no such independent source of necessity, then there would be no necessary objects. But as we have already seen, there must be some necessary objects.

1.4 The Eternity of the World

Aquinas's three cosmological arguments certainly accord with Scripture in affirming that the world began to exist at some time.

> If we suppose, in agreement with the Catholic faith and contrary to what some philosophers have mistakenly thought, that the world has not existed eternally, and that its duration has a beginning, as Holy Scripture which cannot deceive attests, a doubt arises as to whether it could not always have been. (Aquinas, 1998: 713)

There is nonetheless a fascinating discussion of the mere possibility of the world's eternality in *On the Eternity of the World*. Aquinas argues that it is indeed possible that the world is eternal – though it's not actually eternal – but impossible that it could have been eternal and uncaused by God.

Aquinas argues that causes need not temporally precede their effects, so the fact that the world was caused does not entail that its duration is not eternal. Causes precede effects in the order of nature, but not in the order of time.

> It is clear, then, that it is not incoherent to say that an efficient cause need not precede its effect in duration: if it were conceptually

incoherent, God could not of course bring it about. ... It remains to be seen whether it is repugnant to reason that something made should always exist because as a thing made from nothing it is necessary that non-existence precede its duration. (Aquinas, 1998: 714)

Aquinas argues further that it's false in the order of time that the nonexistence of a created object must precede the existence of that object. It is not true that something that comes to be must at some time not be.

[F]or it is not maintained that, if the creature always was, at some time it was nothing, but rather that its nature is such that it would be nothing if left to itself. (Aquinas, 1998: 717)

Creatures that come to be from all eternity are beings that come to be *ex nihilo* at no particular time. The order of existence to nonexistence of created objects is the order of nature. The nonexistence of created objects precedes the existence of created objects only in the sense that these objects would be nothing if they hadn't been caused to exist.

Aquinas's discussion is particularly interesting in its convergence with Leibniz's discussion on the same point.

[E]ven if we assume the past eternity of the world, we can't escape the ultimate and out-of-the-world reason for things, namely God. ... The reasons for the world, therefore, lie hidden in something outside the world, something different from the chain of states or series of things that jointly constitute the world. And so we must move from physical or hypothetical necessity, which determines the later things in the world from the earlier to something that is absolutely or metaphysically necessary, for which a reason can't be given. (Leibniz, 1989a: 149ff.)[11]

Even on the assumption of the eternity of the world, according to Leibniz, the world must have some explanation. It is not central to the cosmological argument that the world begins to exist at some particular time.

---

[11] Similar versions are in Leibniz (1973: secs. 36–38) and Leibniz (1996: secs. 36–37, 44–45, 49–52, 121–122).

The kalām cosmological argument, in contrast, maintains that there is no objective becoming – the world or universe did not objectively or absolutely come to be – if there was no temporal beginning of the world. Since the principle of causation requires an explanation for objects that objectively come to be, it is central to the kalām cosmological argument that the universe had a temporal beginning.

Section 2   The Kalām Cosmological Argument

The kalām cosmological argument has its origin in early Christian theologians who aimed to rebut the Aristotelian doctrine of the eternity of the universe. These arguments in defense of creation *ex nihilo* initiated a long tradition of arguments against an infinite causal history of the universe.[12] Arguments in this tradition were of course much improved by medieval Muslim theologians – hence the Arabic name "kalām" for one powerful version of this sort of argument – and reintroduced to Christian scholastics via Jewish theologians in Muslim Spain. The long debate on the kalām includes disputants of no lesser philosophical prominence than Saadia ben Gaon and Maimonides, al-Ghazali and ibn Rushd, and Bonaventure and Aquinas (Craig and Sinclair, 2012).

The kalām cosmological argument's most prominent contemporary expositor and defender is William Lane Craig, but a vast literature on the argument has emerged since Stuart Hackett's *The Resurrection of Theism*.[13] Much of the literature against the soundness of the kalām has been as illuminating as the ingenious argumentation in favor of the argument. Argumentation on the nature of the infinite has been particularly fascinating. There has been, in addition, empirical evidence concerning the kalām from contemporary astrophysical

---

[12] See Craig and Sinclair (2012). For more historical discussion, see Philoponus (1987) and Philoponus and Simplicius (1987). See also Craig (2001) and Wolfson (1966, 1976).

[13] See in particular Craig (1979, 2001). See also Hackett (1957).

cosmology. There is some evidence for the finitude of the past in contemporary cosmology, but there's also evidence for the coherence of an infinite past. None of this evidence is decisive, certainly.

William Lane Craig offers a version of the kalām cosmological argument originally developed by Muslim theologian al-Ghazali (Al-Ghazali, 1962).[14] The argument is a simple syllogism.

1. Everything that begins to exist has a cause.
2. The universe began to exist.
3. Therefore, the universe has a cause.

The simplicity of the kalām cosmological argument is deceptive. Though an apparently uncontroversial conclusion seems to follow straightforwardly from two innocuous premises, the debate over the soundness of the kalām cosmological argument continues.

According to William Lane Craig, the conclusion of the kalām is not a comparatively small point about causation, but an extremely important metaphysical fact about the provenance of the universe.

> From the two premises, it follows logically that the universe has a cause. This is a staggering conclusion, for it implies that the universe was brought into existence by a transcendent reality. (Craig and Sinclair, 2012: 190)

Setting aside the possibility of genuine self-causation, the conclusion of the kalām entails that something metaphysically prior to the universe is the cause of the universe. Craig argues further that the transcendental cause – the "ultramundane cause" – exemplifies attributes of a divine being. These properties include being the first cause, a person, immaterial, timeless, spaceless, beginningless, uncaused, and enormously powerful.

In discussion of the conclusion Craig and Sinclair remark:

> This, as Thomas Aquinas was wont to remark, is what everybody means by "God." (Craig and Sinclair, 2012: 194)

---

[14] See also Al-Ghazali (1963).

2.1 Initial Problems for Premise (1)

The validity of the kalām cosmological argument is undeniable, and its conclusion has serious theological implications. The premises of the kalām have therefore elicited some elaborate and ingenious argumentation. Perhaps because it appears obviously true, premise (1) has received less philosophical defense. Craig observes concerning premise (1):

> The first step is so intuitively obvious that I think scarcely anyone could sincerely believe it to be false. I therefore think it is somewhat unwise to argue in favor of it, for any proof of the principle is likely to be less obvious than the principle itself. (Craig, 1998)[15]

But Craig does note J. L. Mackie's Humean objection that there is no good a priori reason in favor of (1).

> [W]e can certainly conceive an uncaused beginning-to-be of an object; if what we can thus conceive is nevertheless in some way impossible, this still requires to be shown. (Craig, 1998: 25)

Craig's response is that Hume's argument simply does not make it plausible to think that something could really come into being without a cause. Imagining a horse coming into being from nothing in no way proves that a horse really could come into existence that way.

> The defender of the kalām argument is claiming that it is *really* impossible for something to come uncaused from nothing. Does Mackie sincerely believe that things can pop into existence uncaused, out of nothing? Does anyone in his right mind really believe that, say, a raging tiger could suddenly come into existence uncaused, out of nothing, in this room right now? The same applies to the universe: if prior to the existence of the universe, there was absolutely nothing – no God, no space, no time – how could the universe possibly have come to exist? (Craig, 1998: 25ff.).

---

[15] But see also Craig and Moreland (2015).

There are a number of puzzling statements in this passage. What does the peculiar modal claim mean that it is *really* impossible for something to come uncaused from nothing? If there is some difference between something's being really impossible and something's being impossible, then what exactly is that difference? There are similar worries forthcoming for understanding the modal claim that "actual infinities are impossible." Is there some important difference between the view that actual infinites are impossible and the view that infinites are impossible? If so, that important distinction is hard to make out.

But consider the question "does anyone in his right mind really believe that, say, a raging tiger could suddenly come into existence uncaused, out of nothing, in this room right now?" The question misleadingly conflates having no causal explanation with having no explanation at all. It is not difficult to imagine a causally lawless world – a world that includes no universal laws and no stochastic laws – that is nonetheless not a chaotic world. Let w be a possible world in which B's follow A's during the first epoch of that world, B's follow A's 99.98999 . . .% of the time in the second epoch, B's follow A's 99.998999 . . .% of the time in the third epoch, and so on for infinitely many epochs. It is not a universal law in w that B's follow A's and it is not a stochastic law in w that B's follow A's. It is not an exceptionless regularity that B's follow A's. And the probability that a B event will follow an A event varies over time, indeed there are infinitely many variations in the probability that a B event follows an A event. So there are no stochastic laws that B's follow A's. There is therefore no causal relation between the occurrence of an A event and the occurrence of a B event. Nonetheless, the relationship between A events and B events is not chaotic, either.

In each epoch in w – and epochs of course can vary in duration – we can accurately predict the probability that a B event will occur given that an A event has occurred. The quasi-laws that govern epochs are not causal laws, but they do order the epochs in a quasi-causal way. The possible world w is very orderly, indeed there needn't be any perceivable variation in the behavior of objects. But the orderly world w is one in which there are no causal laws and no causal relations. There are nonetheless quasi-causal explanations for the occurrences of events in w. It is true in w that horses do not come into existence suddenly from nothing, but horses do come into existence without causal explanation. Things do "pop" into existence uncaused in w, but that's only because everything that comes into existence according to quasi-causal laws "pops" into existence uncaused. There are no causal explanations available for anything that comes into existence in w, but there are quasi-causal explanations. Worlds like w show that our alternatives are not causal worlds or chaotic worlds. It is false that every causally lawless world is one in which there are no explanations at all for what occurs in them.

The examples of horses or raging tigers popping into existence uncaused, from nothing, give us no reason to believe that objects cannot come into existence uncaused. For all we really know, our world is one in which what we believe are the causal laws are statistical generalizations whose probabilities oscillate imperceptibly every 100 million years. There would in that case be no evidence that our world is a causally lawless world, but it would be a causally lawless world. And of course, no one in his right mind would believe that raging tigers come into existence from nothing into this room right now. Still, it would be true that tigers come into existence uncaused every time they come into existence at all.

There is also reason to believe that premise (1) is false from the possibility of libertarian freedom. Many theists endorse a form of *source libertarianism* according to which an agent is free only if the agent is the source of (the cause of) her actions.[16] Consider the event of S freely choosing to do A. The cause of A is S, and there is nothing that causes S to cause A. S's causing A is an event that comes into existence uncaused. So according to source libertarianism it is perfectly possible that some things come into existence uncaused. But then it is not necessary that everything that begins to

---

[16] W. L. Craig seems to endorse a form of source libertarianism. See, for instance, *Reasonable Faith*, www.reasonablefaith.org/Free-Will.

exist has a cause. So, there's fairly good reason to believe that premise (1) is false.

But suppose the proper interpretation of premise (1) is as a principle restricting how *objects* might come into existence, rather than restricting how events or actions might come into existence. In this case, then, the orderly lawless worlds described earlier are sufficient to show that, possibly, objects come into existence uncaused.[17] There are no true, universal, non-accidental generalizations in those worlds and there are no true stochastic generalizations in those worlds. There simply are no causal laws at all in those worlds. So, every object comes into existence uncaused in those worlds.[18]

2.2 Kalām and Premise (2)

The philosophical arguments in favor of premise (2) are arguments for the impossibility of an infinite temporal regress of events. The reasoning is that if there cannot be an infinite temporal regress of events, then the actual universe has to have a finite temporal beginning. But the philosophical argument for the proposition that an infinite temporal regress of events cannot exist rests on the metaphysically puzzling claim that there *an actual infinite cannot exist*.

It was the work of Georg Cantor (1915) that largely established the legitimacy of the actual infinite among almost all current and contemporary mathematicians. Indeed, current set theoretical investigations – that is, most mathematical investigations – take as established the existence of sets of transfinite cardinality. Cantor's set theoretical paradise includes a hierarchy of infinite sets beginning with the smallest infinite set $\aleph_0$ and moving upward $\aleph_1, \aleph_2, \aleph_3, \ldots$ and so on infinitely. There are indeed infinitely many sets in Cantor's paradise of larger and larger infinite size or cardinality (Hilbert, 1964).

---

[17] See Bird (2005, 2007), Corry (2011).
[18] Yujin Nagasawa suggested restricting premise (1) in this way.

The defining feature of infinite sets is that they are sets R whose cardinality is equal to some proper subset of R. Two sets R and S have the same size cardinality just in case they are equipollent or there is a one-to-one correspondence between their elements or members.[19] The idea is simple for finite sets. The set {a, b, c} has the same size or cardinality as the set {1, 2, 3} since we can match up each member of the first set with a distinct member of the second set, and vice versa. But necessarily no subset S of a finite set R is equipollent to R. Illustrations abound: {a, b} is obviously not the same size as {a, b, c}.

The idea is somewhat less simple for the infinite sets R = {1, 2, 3, 4 ...} and S = {2, 4, 6, 8 ...} since S is a proper subset of R and yet R and S are equipollent. We can match up every member of R with a distinct member of S and vice versa. R and S therefore have the same size or cardinality, despite the fact that R includes all of the members of S and some members that are not in S. It's of no avail that there are also infinitely many different proper subsets of R that are also equipollent to S. The fact remains that R and S are the same size.

According to William Lane Craig, the view that actual infinites are impossible is the view that actual infinites are metaphysically impossible. But what does this peculiar modal claim mean? Any modal claim of the form "p is impossible" means that p is incompossible with some set of facts (Lewis, 1976: 150). What, then, about the proposition that it is impossible that actually p? If it means that p is incompossible with the *actual facts*, then that is just to say that p is false. But then Craig's claim that actual infinities are metaphysically impossible amounts to nothing more than the claim that it happens to be false that there is an actual infinite. And there is some reason to believe this is what he has in mind.

> Premise [(2)] [an actual infinite cannot exist] asserts that an actual infinite cannot exist in the real world. (Craig and Sinclair, 2012: 103)

---

[19] Two sets S and S' are said to be equipollent if there is a one-to-one correspondence (or a bijection) from S onto S'.

That of course makes the proposition that actual infinites are metaphysically impossible a contingent fact that scientific inquiry ought to resolve. If that is what is meant, then it is extremely misleading to talk about the metaphysical impossibility of actual infinities.

But perhaps the claim that an actual infinity is metaphysically impossible is asserting that the existence of an actual infinity is incompossible with certain actual facts and not others. It is not merely that no actual infinities exist, but that certain facts about the actual world are inconsistent with the existence of an actual infinity. Again, if that is what is meant, then it is extremely misleading to talk about the metaphysical impossibility of actual infinities.

It might also be true that Craig is using "actual" in a secondary, non-rigid, or *shifty* sense (Lewis, 1983b: 22ff.). If so, then that actual infinities are metaphysically impossible is just equivalent to that infinite sequences are metaphysically impossible. No contingent feature of the actual world is incompossible with infinite sequences. Rather no infinite sequences exist in any possible world. This of course is a proper sense in which actual infinites are metaphysically impossible, but it is not entirely obvious that Craig is advancing this thesis.

Metaphysical possibility is sometimes construed as more *narrow* than logical possibility – there are more propositions that are logically possible than are metaphysically possible. For instance, it is not metaphysically possible that your desk should have had a different origin – or so say some famous metaphysicians – but it is logically possible. Metaphysical necessity is correspondingly more *broad* than logical necessity. There are more propositions that are metaphysically necessary than are logically necessary. For instance, it is metaphysically necessary that water is composed of H_2O, but it is not logically necessary.

This characterization of metaphysical and logical possibility is at least unhelpful. To say that a proposition is logically possible is just to say that it is consistent with the logical laws. But there's no such thing as *the* logical laws. Which laws do we take as the touchstone? There is no metaphysical neutrality among logical systems. Logical systems that include the Barcan formulas, for instance, entail that every possible world has the same domain. It's obviously not metaphysically neutral to entail that everything exists necessarily. But classical logics entail that something exists – there are no empty domains – and so classical logic is also not metaphysically neutral.

Should we take the laws of classical logic as the touchstone or the laws of some nonclassical logic? Should we take the laws of some extension of classical logic? Is the touchstone S2, S3, S4, or S5, or some logic in between these, or some temporal logic, or a logic yet to be developed? Whether any distinction exists at all between metaphysical and logical possibility depends entirely on the logic we have in mind. Further, any logic we might adopt will involve metaphysical commitments that are not neutral.

The proposition that actual infinities are metaphysically impossible is difficult to assess. If the proposition is consistent with any particular set of logical laws, it does not follow that the proposition is metaphysically possible. We should add that the fact that the proposition is inconsistent with some law of some logic does not entail that it is metaphysically impossible. Nevertheless we do not have to rely solely on rational intuition to determine whether actual infinities are metaphysically impossible. Several arguments have been advanced for that thesis. And those arguments are certainly open to critical assessment.

One immediate difficulty with the view that actual infinities are impossible is that Georg Cantor showed – to the satisfaction of almost every mathematician – that actual infinities are possible, and indeed indispensable. Craig's response to this well-known fact is that quantification in mathematics is not ontologically committing.

> The Realist, then, if he is to maintain that mathematical objects furnish a decisive counterexample to the denial of the existence of the actual infinite, must provide some overriding argument for the reality of mathematical objects, as well as rebutting defeaters of all the alternatives consistent with classical mathematics – a task

whose prospects for success are dim indeed. It is therefore open to the *mutakallim* to hold that while the actual infinite is a fruitful and consistent concept within the postulated universe of discourse, it cannot be transposed into the real world. (Craig and Sinclair, 2012: 108)

It obviously sets the bar too high to insist that the realist show that mathematical objects exist. The realist believes they do, of course, and that realism is the best mathematical metaphysics. But the realist's contribution to the current discussion need only be that realism about mathematical objects is one possible view available to mathematicians and philosophers of mathematics. Those who maintain that realism is not among the genuine alternatives open to philosophers of mathematics need to offer reasons to believe that mathematical objects are *necessarily nonexistent* – a task whose prospects for success, to quote a phrase, are dim indeed. If such mathematical objects are, for all we know, possible, then we have prima facie reason to believe the matter is settled concerning the metaphysical possibility of actual infinites.

2.3   Actual Infinites and Contradictions

The best way to support [(2)] [an actual infinite cannot exist] is by way of thought experiments that illustrate the various absurdities that would result if an actual infinite were to be instantiated in the real world. [José] Benardete, who is especially creative and effective at concocting such thought experiments, puts it well: "Viewed *in abstracto*, there is no logical contradiction involved in any of these enormities; but we have only to confront them *in concreto* for their outrageous absurdity to strike us full in the face."

(Benardete, 1964: 238)

It is an important question whether any interesting metaphysical conclusions can be drawn from the kinds of scenarios José Benardete describes. Benardete does not offer those scenarios as examples of the metaphysically impossible from which we should draw no conclusions at all. But there are examples of the sort

Benardete describes that seem to generate contradictions. A particularly interesting example is J. F. Thomson's famous lamp. About Thomson's example, Paul Benacerraf notes:

> Thomson's first argument, concerning the lamp, is short, imaginative, and compelling. It appears to demonstrate that "completing a super-task" is a self-contradictory concept. Let me reproduce it here:
>
>> There are certain reading-lamps that have a button in the base. If the lamp is off and you press the button the lamp goes on, and if the lamp is on and you press the button the lamp goes off. So if the lamp was originally off, and you pressed the button an odd number of times, the lamp is on, and if you pressed the button an even number of times the lamp is off. Suppose now that the lamp is off, and I succeed in pressing the button an infinite number of times, perhaps making one jab in one minute, another jab in the next half-minute, and so on. ... After I have completed the whole infinite sequence of jabs, i.e. at the end of the two minutes, is the lamp on or off? It seems impossible to answer this question. It cannot be on, because I did not even turn it on without at once turning it off. It cannot be off, because I did in the first place turn it on, and thereafter I never turned it off without at once turning it on. But the lamp must be either on or off. This is a contradiction. (Benacerraf, 1962: 767)[20]

In fact, there is no contradiction. As Benacerraf shows, there's a straightforward solution to the paradox.

> Thompson's instructions do not cover the state of the lamp at tl, although they do tell us what will be its state at every instant between t0 and t1 (including t0). Certainly, the lamp must be on or off (provided that it hasn't gone up in a meta-physical puff of smoke in the interval), but nothing we are told implies which it is to be. The arguments to the effect that it can't be either have no

---

[20] See also Thomson (1954).

bearing on the case. To suppose that they do is to suppose that a description of the physical state of the lamp at t1 (with respect to its being on or off) is a logical consequence of its state (with respect to the same property) at times prior to t1. (Benacerraf, 1962: 766).

The argument is invalid. Effectively, Thomson's premises apply to instants prior to t1. It is only then that there's no instant that the lamp was on (off) that is not followed by an instant at which it was off (on). Nothing is said about the lamp at t1 or later. The case at t1 is underdetermined.

Hilbert's Paradox of the Grand Hotel has similarly paradoxical consequences. The example is due to mathematician David Hilbert and describes a hotel with infinitely many rooms and infinitely many guests (Hilbert, 1964).[21]

Hilbert's Hotel is even stranger than the German mathematician made it out to be. For suppose some of the guests start to check out. Suppose the guest in room #1 departs. Is there not now one fewer person in the hotel? Not according to infinite set theory! Suppose the guests in rooms #1, 3, 5, ... check out. In this case an infinite number of people has left the hotel, but by Hume's Principle, there are no fewer people in the hotel. In fact, we could have every other guest check out of the hotel and repeat this process infinitely many times, and yet there would never be any fewer people in the hotel. Now suppose the proprietor does not like having a half-empty hotel (it looks bad for business). No matter! By shifting guests in even-numbered rooms into rooms with numbers half their respective room numbers, he transforms his half-vacant hotel into one that is completely full. In fact, if the manager wanted double occupancy in each room, he would have no need of additional guests at all. [But] suppose that the persons in rooms #4, 5, 6, ... checked out. At a single stroke the hotel would be virtually emptied, the guest register reduced to three names, and the infinite converted to finitude. And yet it would remain true that as many guests checked out this time as when the guests in rooms #1, 3, 5, ... checked out!

---

[21] See also Gamow (1946).

> Can anyone believe that such a hotel could exist in reality? (Craig and Sinclair, 2012: 109)

The question of course is not whether anyone could believe that such a hotel could exist in reality, but whether such a hotel is metaphysically possible. The problem illustrated in Hilbert's hotel, according to Craig, is the problem of applying inverse operations on infinite cardinalities. The application of inverse operations, we're told, generates a contradiction.

> [T]he contradiction lies in the fact that one can subtract equal quantities from equal quantities and arrive at different answers. For example, if we subtract all the even numbers from all the natural numbers, we get an infinity of numbers, and if we subtract all the numbers greater than three from all the natural numbers, we get only four numbers. Yet in both cases we subtracted the *identical number* of numbers from the *identical number* of numbers and yet did not arrive at an identical result. In fact, one can subtract equal quantities from equal quantities and get any quantity between zero and infinity as the remainder. For this reason, subtraction and division of infinite quantities are simply prohibited in transfinite arithmetic – a mere stipulation which has no force in the nonmathematical realm. (Craig and Sinclair, 2012: 112)

But how exactly do we get a contradiction? The inference seems to be the following.

(i) $\aleph_n = \aleph_n$ Assumption

(ii) $(\aleph_n = \aleph_n) \longrightarrow (\forall x)((\aleph_n - x) = (\aleph_n - x))$ P1

(iii) $\sim(\forall x)((\aleph_n - x) = (\aleph_n - x))$ Fact

(iv) $\sim(\aleph_n = \aleph_n)$ 3,2 Contradiction

What is the motivation for P1? According to Craig, subtracting identical quantities from identical quantities we should find identical differences. The principle of arithmetic in (ii) is true for domains of finite numbers, but false when x is transfinite. One natural response is to restrict the principle to finite x, but Craig observes that restricting the principle cannot keep people from checking out of the hotel in infinite numbers.

But in reality, one cannot stop people from checking out of a hotel if they so desire! In this case, one does wind up with logically impossible situations, such as subtracting identical quantities from identical quantities and finding non-identical differences. (Craig and Sinclair, 2012: 111–112)

But of course we can generate a contradiction in a similar way for transfinite addition. The problem given earlier has nothing specifically to do with applying inverse operations.

(i') $a \neq b$ Assumption

(ii') $(\forall x)(\forall y)(((\aleph_n + x) = (\aleph_n + y)) \rightarrow (x = y))$ P2

(iii') $(\aleph_n + a) = (\aleph_n + b)$ Fact

(iv') $a = b$ 3,2 Contradiction

What is the motivation for P2? Adding nonidentical numbers to identical numbers yields nonidentical sums. The principle in (ii') holds for all transfinite x and y, but it generates a contradiction for finite x and y. There are of course diverse, finite a and b such that $(\aleph_n + a) = (\aleph_n + b)$. Do we conclude that there are no finite numbers in the "real world"? This seems like an absurd response to the puzzle. Maybe we should restrict principle P2 to infinite x and y. Of course, in reality, to paraphrase Craig, we cannot stop people from checking into the Hilbert hotel in finite numbers. Right, but checking into the hotel in finite numbers should not yield a contradiction and checking out of a hotel in infinite numbers should not yield a contradiction. Those contradictions are avoided provided the domains of the principles P1 and P2 are properly restricted. Quantifiers in (ii) should be restricted to the domain of finite numbers, and the quantifiers in (ii') should be restricted to the domain of the transfinite.

2.4 From the Grim Reaper to the Kalām

Another example of infinite sequences with paradoxical consequences is the Grim Reaper paradox. David Chalmers describes the classic Grim Reaper this way.

> There are countably many grim reapers, one for every positive integer. Grim reaper 1 is disposed to kill you with a scythe at 1 pm, if and only if you are still alive then (otherwise his scythe remains immobile throughout), taking 30 minutes about it. Grim reaper 2 is disposed to kill you with a scythe at 12:30 pm, if and only if you are still alive then, taking 15 minutes about it. Grim reaper 3 is disposed to kill you with a scythe at 12:15 pm, and so on. You are still alive just before 12 pm, you can only die through the motion of a grim reaper's scythe, and once dead you stay dead. (Chalmers, 2000: 155)

José Benardete claimed that the serrated infinities in the Grim Reaper paradox exhibit strange "force fields" that repel objects at a distance.

> What happens now if we undertake to crash into the open end of the boards. [S]eeing that each board is effectively shielded by its successor, it is evident that, although we shall be able to approach indefinitely close to the open end, there is a point beyond which we cannot pass: the ne plus ultra. Not that we shall be repelled by contact with anyone of the boards. No. The infinite sequence logically entails what we may describe as a field of force which shuts us out from further advance. (Benardete, 1964: 258)

John Hawthorne claims that it is a consequence of the Grim Reaper that a fusion of assassins might bring about the death of the ill-fated Bob without actually doing anything.

> [T]he assassin fusion seems to accomplish effect c without doing anything at all. . . . So it follows that the fusion causally secures the assassination of Bob without even moving! (Hawthorne, 2000: 630)

Alex Pruss and Robert Koons claim that it is a consequence of the Grim Reaper paradox that an infinite sequence of past events cannot exist. The actual past is therefore finite. Pruss argues that if there could be a backwardly infinite sequence of events, then the Grim Reaper paradox would be possible. Since the Grim Reaper paradox cannot happen, there cannot be a backwardly infinite sequence of events (Pruss, 2009).[22]

---

[22] See also Koons (2014).

In fact, the Grim Reaper has none of these fascinating metaphysical consequences. There's nothing about an infinite number of assassins or an infinite sequence of events or an infinite number of instants of time or points of space that is essential to the formulation of a Grim Reaper. We can formulate a single assassin Grim Reaper that makes none of these assumptions. The central problem exhibited in the Grim Reaper is that the assassin is given an impossible task. Grim Reapers are therefore impossible. The right conclusion is that Grim Reapers entail no interesting metaphysical consequences.

As we have noted, nothing about the Grim Reaper paradox requires an infinite number of assassins. Suppose x and y stand for points on a stopwatch such that $y > x$. Now, suppose there is a single assassin who kills Bob at time $\frac{1}{2}(y - x)$, if Bob is still alive. We assume it is causally impossible for Bob to survive the assassin at $\frac{1}{2}(y - x)$. Next we assume that the assassin kills Bob at $\frac{1}{4}(y - x)$, if Bob is still alive. Next we assume that the assassin kills Bob at $1/8(y - x)$, if Bob is still alive. And of course for each finite natural n, the assassin kills Bob at each time $1/2^n(y - x)$ seconds, if Bob is still alive. Each division can of course be taken as either a temporal or a spatial division, either a spatial division on the stopwatch or a division in time.[23]

We do not assume that any interval has been infinitely divided or that any time is composed of infinitely many instants. We do not assume that space or time is infinitely divided or composed of infinitely many points or instants. So we make no assumptions concerning an actual infinite. We do assume that for any finite division of the interval $1/2^n(y - x)$ there is possible another finite division of the interval $1/2^{n+1}(y - x)$.

The stopwatch is not suddenly destroyed before $\frac{1}{2}(y - x)$ and Bob is not killed before $\frac{1}{2}(y - x)$. We assume that the stopwatch is started. Suppose for reductio that for some time $1/2^n(y - x)$ there is no earlier time

---

[23] Thanks to Graham Oppy for an informative discussion of single-assassin Grim Reapers.

$1/2^{n+j}(y-x)$ at which the assassin kills Bob. If so, then Bob has survived the assassin at some earlier time $1/2^{n+j}(y-x)$. But by hypothesis Bob is not killed before time $1/2^n(y-x)$ and Bob cannot survive the assassin at any time in the interval. So, the assumption for reductio is false and (1) is true.

1. For all n, there's some j, such that the assassin kills Bob at $1/2^{n+j}(y-x)$.

    For each time in the interval the assassin kills Bob at some earlier time in the interval. But if the assassin kills Bob before *each* time in the interval, then there is no time n in the interval at which the assassin kills Bob. For any time $1/2^n(y-x)$ at which the assassin might kill Bob, the assassin has killed Bob at some earlier time $1/2^{n+j}(y-x)$. So, (2) must also be true.

2. For some n, there is no j, such that the assassin kills Bob at $1/2^{n+j}(y-x)$.

    If (2) is true, then (1) is false. But (1) entails (2). So, if (1) is true, then (1) is false. Therefore (1) is false.

The problem that Grim Reapers exhibit has nothing to do with the assumption that there are actual infinites. The problem can be generated without assuming that there are infinitely many Grim Reapers, or infinitely many instants of time or infinitely many points of space. The problem exhibited in the Grim Reaper paradox is that the Grim Reaper is given instructions that are impossible to fulfill. None of the proposed metaphysical conclusions follows from the Grim Reaper.

2.5 Actual Infinites and Successive Addition

Arguments against an actual infinite from successive addition rest on the claim that no collection – no collection of objects, events, states of affairs, etc. – formed by successive addition can be an actual infinite. Collections formed by successive addition are just those collections formed by adding one item after another to form a set of items. If an actual infinite cannot be formed by successive addition, then the series of past events must be finite. According to the argument, the series of past events is formed by successive addition of one event after another in a temporal sequence.

But why can't an actual infinite be formed by successive addition? What exactly is the argument?

> The impossibility of the formation of an actual infinite by successive addition seems obvious in the case of beginning at some point and trying to reach infinity. For given any finite number n, n + 1 equals a finite number. Hence, $\aleph_0$ has no immediate predecessor; it is not the terminus of the natural number series but stands, as it were, outside it and is the number of all the members in the series. (Craig and Sinclair, 2012: 117–118)

The puzzling aspect of the argument offered earlier is the assumption that we could only count to infinity if $\aleph_0$ had an immediate predecessor. Of course, it is not coherent to speak of $\aleph_0$ having an immediate predecessor, since it isn't an ordinal number. The difficulty in forming an actual infinite by successive addition, then, is alleged to be the fact that for each n in the series of natural numbers n + 1 is a finite number. That is to say, for each n in the series of natural numbers that we might reach, we never find an n + 1 that is an infinite number.

It is difficult to see the aim of the argument. It is of course true that every number in the series of natural numbers is finite, and so it is of course true that for each n in the series of naturals n + 1 is a finite number. If we count to the end of the natural numbers – the smallest infinite set of numbers – we will have counted only finite numbers. We will not have reached a number named '$\aleph_0$'. It is perhaps a strange mathematical fact that in order to count the smallest infinity quantity we need only count finite numbers – we must count all of the finite positive integers – but *nothing beyond* finite positive integers. But that's not quite right. We needn't count all of the positive integers; we need only count the positive *even* integers. And of course that's not quite right either. We need only count every other positive even integer, or every third positive even integer, and so on.

Let S1 = {t1, t2, t3, . . ., t1000}, let S2 = {t1, t2, t3, . . ., t1000, t1001, t1002, t1003, . . ., t2000}, S3 = {t1, t2, t3, . . ., t1000, t1001, t1002, t1003, . . ., t2000, t2001, t2002, t2003, . . ., t3000}, and so on for each Sn, n ≥ 1. For each finite Sn there is an Sn +1 that is also finite, for every positive integer n. *Every set Sn is finite.* Could there be a clock that ticks off one second for each time in S1? Certainly, that is possible, since S1 is finite. Could the clock tick off all of the seconds in S2? S2 is S1 with the addition of finitely many more times, so certainly a clock could tick off the seconds in S2. Could it tick off the seconds in S3? Of course it could, since again it's a finite series. Now consider the inductive hypothesis, for mathematical induction, that for any finite Sn in the series, the clock could tick off all of the times in Sn + 1. That of course is also true, since every Sn is finite. So, given the basis step and the inductive hypothesis, we can conclude that the clock could tick off the times in every finite set Sn. But if the clock could tick off the times in every finite set, then it could tick off every finite time.

Now it might be considered an objection to the argument that the clock only ticks off finite times in each Sn. Thus, Craig:

> Do Mackie and Sobel think that because every finite segment of the series can be formed by successive addition the whole infinite series can be so formed? That is as logically fallacious as saying that because every part of an elephant is light in weight, the whole elephant is light in weight, or in other words, to commit the fallacy of composition. (Craig and Sinclair, 2012: 110)

Mathematical induction is valid. If 1 has the property of being a number, and if for each finite n, if n is a number, then n + 1 is a number, then all of the positive integers are numbers. Likewise, if n is traversed, and if for each finite n, if n is traversed, then n + 1 is traversed, then all of the positive integers are traversed. Yes, the *whole thing!* No fallacy of composition is involved. The mistake is in believing that we would have to traverse something other than finite numbers in order to traverse an infinite series.

But it might be urged that, no matter how much the clock ticks, the clock never reaches an infinite time $t_{\aleph_0}$. But this is just confused. It is true that the clock only ticks off finite times in each Sn. And it is also true that the clock never reaches the infinite time $t_{\aleph_0}$. But this is because *no such time* as $t_{\aleph_0}$ exists. If the clock ticks off the finite times in each Sn – as we have proven it does by mathematical induction – then the clock ticks off infinitely many times. It ticks off infinitely many times without ever ticking off $t_{\aleph_0}$. It ticks off infinitely many times without ever ticking off anything but finite times.

> Notice that the impossibility of forming an actual infinite by successive addition has nothing to do with the amount of time available. Sometimes it is wrongly alleged that the only reason an actual infinite cannot be formed by successive addition is because there is not enough time. But this is mistaken. While we can imagine an actually infinite series of events mapped onto a tenselessly existing infinite series of temporal intervals, such that each consecutive event is correlated with a unique consecutive interval, the question remains whether such a sequence of intervals can be instantiated, not tenselessly, but one interval after another. The very nature of the actual infinite precludes this. For regardless of the time available, a potential infinite cannot be turned into an actual infinite by any amount of successive addition since the result of every addition will always be finite. (Craig and Sinclair, 2012: 122)

But of course finite temporal intervals can be mapped onto a single possible world consecutively. Consider an infinite series of possible worlds w1, w2, w3, . . ., wn, in which a clock ticks off the times in the finite sets S1, S2, S3, . . ., Sn, respectively. It is true that there is no possible world in the series in which every finite time is ticked off. But there is also a possible world w' that includes as world stages ws1, ws2, ws3, . . ., wsn where ws1 is temporally isomorphic to w1 (all of the times ticked off in w1 are ticked off in world stage ws1), ws2 is temporally isomorphic to w2, ws3 is temporally isomorphic to w3, and so on. Each world stage wsn includes a finite set of times ticked off consecutively. There is no problem about ticking off a finite number of times consecutively. Every time that is ticked off in world w' is finite. No time that is ticked off in w' is infinite. It is true in w' that every finite time is ticked off consecutively.

2.6 A-Theory, Block Universes, and Objective Becoming

There is an interesting argument that the universe comes into being objectively – this is the *objective becoming of the universe* – if and only if the A-theory of time is correct. The argument aims to rule out the possibility that a complete tenselessly existing manifold comes into being objectively.

> The past did not spring into being whole and entire but was formed sequentially, one event occurring after another. Notice, too, that the direction of this formation is "forward," in the sense that the collection grows with time. . . . [This premise] presupposes once again an A-Theory of time. On such a theory, the collection of all past events prior to any given event is not a collection whose members all tenselessly coexist. Rather it is a collection that is instantiated sequentially or successively in time, one event coming to pass on the heels of another. Since temporal becoming is an objective feature of the physical world, the series of past events is not a tenselessly existing manifold, all of whose members are equally real. Rather the members of the series come to be and pass away one after another. . . . [W]e take ourselves to be justified in affirming the objective reality of temporal becoming and, hence, the formation of the series of temporal events by successive addition. (Craig and Sinclair, 2012: 124)

According to this argument, temporal becoming is an objective feature of the universe if and only if the series of past events is not a tenselessly existing manifold. And the suggestion is that past events do not constitute a tenselessly existing manifold if and if and only if the A-theory of time is true. Call that the *objective becoming argument*. If the objective becoming argument is sound, then we need a causal explanation for the objective coming to be of the universe if and only if A-theory is true.

The objective becoming argument is, in fact, unsound. It is possible that the past is a tenselessly existing manifold and that the universe comes into existence objectively. It is an important consequence that, whether or not the universe had an infinite past, it requires some (perhaps causal) explanation. It takes us further into cosmological argumentation to observe that, even if the universe exists eternally and necessarily, it does not follow that no causal explanation for the existence of the universe is required.

2.7 Block Theory and Genuine Change

What is the A-theory of time? A-theory is often conflated with various doctrines that some, but not all, A-theorists hold. A-theory is not the view that only the present exists, or that time flows, or that time passes, or that there is genuine or robust change, or that "earlier than" and "later than" must be defined in terms of pastness, presentness, and futurity, and so on. None of these doctrines is essential to the A-theory of time.

According to the A-theory, past, present, and future are intrinsic, monadic properties of things and events. It is an intrinsic property of dinosaurs that they are past, and an intrinsic property of Martian colonies that they are future. These are the intrinsic and monadic "A-properties," and this is the central commitment of A-theory. In contrast, B-theorists deny that there are any A-properties. The B-theory of time replaces the intrinsic monadic A-properties with temporal relations. Call these the "B-relations." The B-relations are "earlier than," "later than," and "simultaneous with," and these are not reducible to the intrinsic, monadic, A-properties.

The argument that there is objective becoming if and only if A-theory is true assumes that, necessarily, if A-theory is true, then the block theory of the universe is false. According to the block theory, the universe is a four-dimensional, tenselessly existing manifold. The universe is an infinite collection of instantaneous three-dimensional spaces. The totality of spatiotemporal reality – past, present, future – all exists in the very same way. The future and the past are not, for instance, maximally consistent sets of sentences or maximal propositions or any other sort of abstract object. Indeed, the past and the future are no less concrete than the present. Dinosaurs exist in the same way that dogs exist. Dogs are concrete objects and so are dinosaurs. The difference is simply a matter of temporal location. Dinosaurs are *back there* in the past and dogs are *right here*. Saturn's space stations exist in the same way as shopping malls. The difference again is a matter of location. Saturn's space stations exist *up there* in the future and shopping malls are right here. There is no absolute past, present, and future on this view. "Past," "present," and "future" are rather indexicals like "here" and "there," so what is past, present, and future varies depending entirely on one's location in the manifold.

A-theory of time does not in fact entail that block theory is false. But let's assume that it does and ask whether (i) the block universe entails that there is no objective becoming and whether (ii) cosmological arguments depend on objective becoming. If the block theory of the universe is true, according to the preceding argument, then there is no objective becoming in the universe. But, why not? The thought is that objective becoming entails genuine change. But there cannot be any genuine change in a block universe. Russell famously argued, on the contrary, that block theory is perfectly compatible with change. The reasoning is simple, a clock in the block universe will indicate 8 at T1 and 10 at T2, and that is a genuine change. But here's McTaggart's response to Russell (Skow, 2015).

> Yes, the clock indicates 8 at T1, but it always indicates 8 at T1. Similarly it always indicates 10 at T2. So, there is no change. (McTaggart, 1927)

The universe is one way at one spatiotemporal location and another way at another spatiotemporal location. But the universe is not genuinely changing. It's analogous, McTaggart noted, to a pencil being one way at one spatial location – say, at the eraser – and another way at another spatial location – say, at the tip. There is no genuine change going on in the pencil given these distinct properties at the erasure and tip, and similarly there is no genuine change going on in the block universe.

There is, perhaps, a more compelling argument that the block universe cannot undergo genuine change. If the block universe U is undergoing genuine change, then U has to exemplify some genuine property F at one time and exemplify another genuine property ~F at another time. But it is impossible that U exemplifies F at time t and that U exemplifies ~F at another time t'. If U exemplifies F at t and U exemplifies ~F at t', then U at t $\neq$ U at t'. This follows from a simple application of Leibniz's law.

But defenders of change in the block universe urge that Leibniz's law does not preclude the possibility that an object changes with respect to its genuine atemporal properties.

> [F]our dimensionalists tend to employ an atemporal notion of exemplication of properties and relations. Thus, a four dimensionalist will say that my current temporal part is, atemporally, sitting, 69 inches tall, and wearing a hat; and a four dimensionalist will say that this temporal part is, atemporally, part of the larger space-time worm that is me. This is not to say that four dimensionalists reject the notion of change. For the four dimensionalist, change is difference between successive temporal parts. I change from sitting to standing, in the intuitive sense of change, because I have a temporal part that sits and a later one that stands. (Sider, 1997)

Change for the four-dimensionalist can seem like magic. We have an object supposedly undergoing change despite having no parts that undergo change. A person stage S has some property F and a subsequent person stage S' has a property ~F. Neither S nor S' undergoes any change, but the sum S + S' does! Since the properties of the parts are genuine – they are not relational properties or relations – no part can itself undergo any genuine change. That again would be a violation of Leibniz's law. And for exactly the same reasons, the whole object cannot have a genuine property F at time t and a genuine property ~F at time t'. That violates Leibniz's law. Instead we have a large four-dimensional object that has one part exemplifying F and a distinct part exemplifying ~F. There is no more genuine change in four-dimensional objects than there is genuine change in McTaggart's pencil.

But if there's no objective becoming in the universe – no genuine change – then, according to the argument given earlier, we lose a crucial assumption in the kalām cosmological argument. We lose the assumption that the universe comes into being objectively, that the temporal series of events from the past to the present is a collection formed by successive addition. But is this assumption crucial to the kalām cosmological argument?

The assumption can seem crucial, since premise (2) in the cosmological argument states that the universe began to exist. But if there is a block universe, it does not follow that the universe did not come into existence. Even if the block universe is "actually infinite," it does not follow that the universe did not come into existence. Indeed, there is as much reason to believe that the universe came into existence on the assumption that we have an actually infinite block universe as we do on the assumption that we have a finite universe that came into existence sequentially.

The assumption can also seem crucial to premise (1) in the kalām cosmological argument. Premise (1) states that everything that begins to exist has a cause. But it is the *contingency* of the universe – not its finitude or ontological structure – that makes premise (1) true. Suppose presentism is true together with A-theory. A-theory and presentism are in fact logically independent. A-theory does not entail presentism and presentism does not entail A-theory (Rasmussen, 2012). According to Craig, a finite, presentist, A-theoretic universe paradigmatically exemplifies objective becoming. But premise (1) might well be false in such a universe. Premise (1) is true only if we make the additional assumption that the universe is contingent.

Recall that Spinoza argued that the world we inhabit is a *necessitarian* world. There is, according to Spinoza, exactly one possible world and therefore, of course, exactly one possible universe. If the actual world is Spinozistic, then there is no contingency at all in the universe, despite how it appears. All possibility is epistemic possibility. Everything happens as a matter of metaphysical necessity, everything exists necessarily, and everything exemplifies its properties – all of its properties – essentially. What is important to observe is that Spinozistic universes are compatible with objective becoming and genuine change. The Spinozistic universe might be temporally finite, come into existence sequentially, and indeed *begin to exist* at some temporal point. But the event of the universe coming into existence occurs as a matter of metaphysical necessity.[24] Premise (2) is true: the universe began to exist. But premise (1) is false. Objects that come into existence as a matter of metaphysical necessity do not have or require a causal explanation. Despite its finitude and objective becoming, the Spinozistic universe lacks all contingency. Since the universe comes into existence as a matter of metaphysical necessity, not as a matter of causal necessity, it is false that everything that comes into existence has a cause. To put the matter another way, the Spinozistic universe essentially comes into being and essentially exists. The explanation for why the universe exists is not a causal explanation. So, again, premise (1) is not true in the Spinozistic universe.

Our central conclusion is that it's neither necessary nor sufficient to establish premise (2) or premise (1) in the kalām cosmological argument that the universe is finite – the past of the universe is actually finite – and that the universe exhibits genuine change and objective becoming. It can be true that a finite universe exhibits genuine change and objective becoming but that the universal has no cause. It does not have a cause because it exists as a matter of metaphysical necessity. It can also be true that an infinite universe exhibits no genuine change or objective becoming, and that the universe does have a cause.

2.8 Cosmology and Premise (2)

The philosophical arguments in favor of premise (2) aim to show that the universe must have had a temporal beginning, since an actual infinite cannot exist. If no actual infinites exist, then no actual infinite past exists. William Lane Craig has offered, in

---

[24] One might not want to call this objective change, since all of the properties of the actual universe are essential to it. I'm sympathetic to this position. The conclusion would then be that objective becoming does not require literal change.

addition to the philosophical arguments, a set of *inductive arguments* for the thesis that there was an actual beginning to the universe.

The inductive arguments appeal to the standard cosmology of the universe commonly called the big bang theory. According to the standard cosmology, the universe came into being a finite time ago.

> The standard big bang model, as the Friedman-Lemaître model came to be called, thus describes a universe that is not eternal in the past but that came into being a finite time ago. Moreover – and this deserves underscoring – the origin it posits is an absolute origin *ex nihilo.* For not only all matter and energy, but space and time itself come into being at the initial cosmological singularity. (Craig and Moreland, 2015: 186ff.)[25]

There are of course competing cosmological accounts of the universe such as the oscillating universe that expands and contracts forever and the chaotic inflationary universe that continually produces new universes. Craig observes that each of these models posits an infinite future, but each of these also posits a finite past. Of course, unless the futures are merely potential infinite and not actually infinite, these cosmological models are a priori impossible on Craig's view.

But there is also the vacuum fluctuation cosmology that posits an eternal vacuum from which our universe is produced. This cosmological model is also a priori impossible on Craig's view. But Craig further objects that, given the eternal vacuum cosmology, we have no explanation for why we do not observe an infinitely old universe.

Other inductive arguments come from principles of thermodynamics. The second law of thermodynamics seems to predict a *heat death* to universes like our own. The problem, according to Craig, is that if the universe were infinite in duration, then it would long ago have undergone a heat death, given the thermodynamic properties of the universe.

[25] See also Craig (1979: 110ff.).

The universe is, on a naturalistic view, a closed system, since it is everything there is and there is nothing outside it. This seems to imply that, given enough time, the universe and all of its processes will run down, and the entire universe will come to equilibrium. This is known as the heat death of the universe. Once the universe reaches this state, no further change is possible. The universe is dead. (Craig and Moreland, 2015: 187ff.)

It is at least curious that the argument assumes that the universe is closed and that there is nothing outside the universe. These are not scientific claims. Rather they are metaphysical claims that it is extremely unlikely a theist would endorse. But setting aside specific worries about these arguments, there are larger problems with the general approach of drawing metaphysical inferences about the structure of the universe from cosmological theories in recent science.

There is a basic concern with the inductive arguments that at least some big bang theorists are eternalists. The two views are consistent, and there are various versions. Eternalists are in general B-theorists who reject the view that past, present, and future are intrinsic, monadic properties of things and events. It is strictly false on B-theory that the event of the big bang is intrinsically past. Could the entire four-dimensional manifold have come into existence all at once? Certainly it might have – since all time and all space might have come into existence at once – and the four-dimensional manifold might be temporally infinite in both past and future directions. There is no temporal beginning to the universe, on this account, and the big bang did not occur at any temporal point. Since the universe did not come into existence at any temporal point, there is no temporal point at which it was caused to exist. The kalām argument simply does not apply.

The main point is that the inductive facts just do not show that any premise in the cosmological argument is true. The inductive facts require additional philosophical argumentation to establish that there was some temporal beginning to the universe. It has to be shown, inter alia, that the eternalist, B-theorist view of the universe described earlier is false, and that question is not a scientific one.

But note too that it is a metaphysical conclusion – *not* a scientific conclusion – that the universe is a contingent object that came into existence at some finite point in the past. Commonsense epistemology is not transparent relative to the metaphysical structure of the world. Big bang cosmology posits that there was a finite point in the past at which the universe was *concretized*. But it requires an additional inference to reach the conclusion that the point where the universe was concretized was just the point at which the universe came into existence. Scientific investigation can tell us nothing concerning whether concrete objects cease to exist when they become non-concrete. An argument that concrete objects cease to exist when they cease to be concrete would have to address philosophical investigations that have arrived at the conclusion that the universe and everything in it exists necessarily, either concretely or non-concretely (Linsky and Zalta, 1994).[26] It is the philosophical arguments that matter to whether the universe came into existence at some finite time in the past.

Scientific investigation can tell us nothing concerning the modal structure of the world. For all the inductive facts can tell us, we inhabit a modally restricted, Spinozistic world. If we in fact inhabit a Spinozistic world – and any number of theistic multiverse worlds are Spinozistic worlds – then everything that exists, necessarily exists (Kraay, 2010, 2011;Turner, 2003, 2014). Big bang theory is perfectly consistent with every event, fact, and object in the universe occurring, obtaining, or existing as a matter of metaphysical necessity. The unfolding of the universe from the big bang onward tells us absolutely nothing concerning the metaphysical structure of the world. If ours is a Spinozistic world of some sort – say, a theistic multiverse – then there is no causal explanation for the universe or any part of the universe. If the universe came into existence, then it did so as a matter of metaphysical necessity – not causal necessity – and if the universe will go out of existence,

---

[26] See also Williamson (2013).

then it will do so as a matter of metaphysical necessity – not causal necessity. There are no explanations in Spinozistic worlds that we would recognize as causal.

Scientific investigation can tell us nothing concerning whether we inhabit a Ludovician pluriverse. If we inhabit a Ludovician pluriverse, then everything that exists anywhere in the pluriverse, including of course our particular region of it, necessarily exists (Almeida, 2017a, 2017b; Lewis, 1986a). The big bang explanation of our region of the pluriverse is perfectly consistent with every object in the pluriverse existing as a matter of metaphysical necessity and every event – including the big bang – occurring as a matter of metaphysical necessity. If there is an explanation for the totality of the pluriverse then it is not a causal explanation.

The main problems with the scientific arguments are the inferences from empirical facts to metaphysical conclusions. The cosmological evidence for the big bang does not entail that (i) the universe has a temporally finite past, (ii) the universe came into existence at some time in the past, (iii) the universe contains concrete contingent objects, (iv) the universe exists contingently, or (v) the universe has a causal explanation. If it were established that big bang cosmology is true, it would not follow that any of (i)–(v) is true.

To establish any one of (i)–(v) requires philosophical argumentation against the thesis that metaphysical reality is structured in the way many multiverse theorists or Spinozists or necessitists or permanentists or Ludovician theorists claim. Current scientific cosmology can provide no evidence to establish any of (i)–(v).

Section 3   Leibnizian Cosmological Arguments

We have divided cosmological arguments into three sorts or varieties: Thomistic, kalām, and Leibnizian cosmological arguments. Alex Pruss offers a similar taxonomical division.

> There are then three basic kinds of cosmological arguments: Kalam, Thomistic, and Leibnizian. The Kalam and Thomistic arguments

> posit an intuitively plausible Causal Principle (CP) that says that
> every item of some sort – for example, event, contingent being,
> instance of coming-into-existence, or movement – has a cause. ...
> Leibnizian arguments, on the other hand, invoke a very general
> explanatory principle, such as the PSR [principle of sufficient rea-
> son], which is then applied to the cosmos or to some vast cosmic
> state of affairs, or else a nonlocal CP that can be applied to an
> infinite chain or the universe as a whole. (Pruss, 2012)

The explanatory principle in the Leibnizian cosmological argument is the principle of sufficient reason (PSR). It is the distinctive
feature of Leibnizian argument. The principle of sufficient reason
states roughly that everything has an explanation. Spinoza formu-
lates the principle in a useful way.

> For the existence or non-existence of everything there must be
> a reason or cause. For example, if a triangle exists, there must be
> a reason or cause why it exists; but if it does not exist, there must also
> be a reason or cause which hinders its existence or which negates it.
> (Spinoza, 1949: Ip11d)

"Everything" in the broadest version of the principle is an unrestricted quantifier. The items that have explanations are all of the
items that are true or occur or exist or obtain, and everything that is
false or fails to occur, exist, or obtain. These items might include
events, facts, states of affairs, propositions, objects, properties, sets,
classes, and the like. It is an interesting question whether an
explanation is provided for all existing items if an explanation is
provided for all items collected in one's ideology – all of one's
primitive items. But also requiring explanations are various sorts
of logical closures on all existing items. For instance, if propositions
p and q have explanations, then the conjunction of those propositions, p & q, also has an explanation. If the states of affairs or facts
p and q have explanations, then the conjunctive state of affairs, p &
q, has an explanation, and so on.

Most important for Leibnizian cosmological arguments, the totality of metaphysical reality also has an explanation. In addition to the

explanations available for various parts of metaphysical reality, there is an explanation for the *totality of metaphysical reality*. The totality of metaphysical reality, on one view, is the mereological sum of all existing objects – all actualia and all possibilia (if any). Alternatively the totality of metaphysical reality might be a maximally consistent conjunction of true propositions or a maximally consistent conjunctive state of affairs or a maximally consistent property – the complete way that things are. It might also be a single, very large, maximally consistent state of affairs (Divers, 2007).

The unrestricted version of PSR entails that even necessary beings have explanations. According to William Rowe, necessary beings are taken to be self-explanatory beings.

> In stating the first part of the Cosmological Argument we shall make use of . . . the concept of a dependent being and the concept of a self-existent being. By a dependent being we mean a being whose existence is accounted for by the causal activity of other things. . . . By a self-existent being we mean a being whose existence is accounted for by its own nature. This idea . . . is an essential element in the theistic concept of God. (Rowe, 2015: 169ff.)

Necessary beings are self-explanatory, on this account, if and only if existence is part of the nature of that being. Call a being *intrinsically necessary* if and only if the essence of that being involves existence. The self-existent beings that Rowe mentions are intrinsically necessary beings. Intrinsically necessary beings, on this account, require an explanation as much as any other existing beings or items. It is just that the explanation provided is somewhat unusual: the intrinsically necessary beings explain themselves. But, we might reasonably ask, how exactly? Consider Spinoza's answer to what explains God's existence.

> Spinoza explains the necessity of God's existence by appealing to God's nature. This may sound like a non-answer, but it is not. Spinoza is not claiming that there are no explanatory grounds for God's existence; he is claiming that facts about God's nature explain the modality of God's existence. *Self*-explanation, though unusual, is

not identical to *non*-explanation. What about God explains God's existence? ... Spinoza appeals to an involvement relation between the concept of God's essence and the concept of God's existence. That is, God exists in virtue of the fact that the concept of God involves the concept of existence. Spinoza also thinks that the conceptual involvement relation between God and existence explains the fact that God *necessarily* exists. (Newlands, 2013)

Spinoza offers an explanation for why intrinsically necessary beings exist necessarily. A being is intrinsically necessary just in case it is conceptually impossible for that being not to exist. Absolute or metaphysical necessity on this account is explained in terms of conceptual necessity, and the conceptual relationship between the property of existing and the essence of a being is what Spinoza offers to explain why that being necessarily exists.

According to the formulation of the principle of sufficient reason present earlier, the existence of necessary beings requires an explanation. The existence of intrinsically necessary beings is explained conceptually. But there are also *extrinsically necessary* beings. Extrinsically necessary beings are absolutely or metaphysically necessary too, but as Spinoza might put it, the essences of those beings do not involve existence: they are, in short, extrinsically necessary but intrinsically contingent (Griffin, 2013). Among the extrinsically necessary beings we must include, of course, every necessarily existing being that is not intrinsically necessary. But which objects are those?

Both Spinoza and Leibniz argue that everything other than God is extrinsically necessary – every existing object, occurring event, obtaining state of affairs, or fact – and the principle of sufficient reason entails that the existence, occurrence, and obtaining all of these extrinsically necessary beings has an explanation (Griffin, 2013, chs. 2 and 3). Human beings, dogs, stars, leptons, planets, for instance, and the rest of creation are extrinsically necessary. For both Leibniz and Spinoza, the sufficient reason for all extrinsically necessary beings is the exclusively intrinsically necessary being, viz. God. And if X is the sufficient reason or sufficient ground of Y – if X is an explanation for Y that satisfies PSR – then X *entails* Y. If X is genuinely sufficient reason for Y, then it is impossible that the reason X should be true and Y not exist, obtain, or occur.

Metaphysical views according to which everything other than God is extrinsically necessary can seem quaint and wildly inconsistent with contemporary metaphysical commitments. But many contemporary metaphysical views approximate the Leibnizian and Spinozistic picture of metaphysical reality. To begin with a logical consideration, the simplest quantified modal logic (SQML) validates the Barcan formulas. The Barcan formulas entail that everything that exists, necessarily exists (Linsky and Zalta, 1994). SQML has the advantage of showing nicely that, under suitable interpretations, the metaphysical consequences of the Barcan formulas are much less extreme than they might appear. Everything exists necessarily, but as Tim Williamson puts it, "this may not be the view you first thought of."

But we find the view that everything that exists, necessarily exists in Tim Williamson's metaphysical *necessitism* as well.

> Our existence, like most other aspects of our lives, appears frighteningly contingent. It is therefore surprising that there is a proof of my necessary existence, a proof that generalizes to everything whatsoever. (Williamson, 2002: 233)

And of course we find the view that unrestrictedly everything that exists, necessarily exists in David Lewis's account of metaphysical reality.

> Skyrms conjures up the spectre of a regress from a plurality of worlds to a plurality of grand worlds to a plurality of yet grander worlds. ....
> The regress works by cycling around three assumptions: (1) that "reality" is the totality of everything, (2) that reality might have been different, and (3) that possible difference is to be understood in terms of a plurality of alternatives. I reply that (1) and (2) aren't both right. Which one is wrong depends on whether we choose to take "reality" as a blanket term for everything, or as yet another word for the this-worldly part of everything. (Lewis, 1986: 100ff.)

If "reality" is the totality of metaphysical reality, then of course (2) is false. The totality of everything there is – all possibilia and all actualia – could not have been different. It necessarily exists and is necessarily as it is. This of course is an even closer approximation to the metaphysical reality in Leibniz and Spinoza. Everything in the Ludovician pluriverse exists necessarily and has all of its properties essentially, and everything in the Leibnizian and Spinozistic world exists necessarily and has all of its properties as a matter of metaphysical necessity.

3.1　Leibniz on the Cosmological Argument

In *On the Ultimate Origination of Things* Leibniz develops and defends a cosmological argument based on the principle of sufficient reason.

> We can't find in any individual thing, or even in the entire collection and series of things, a sufficient reason why they exist. Suppose that a book on the elements of geometry has always existed, each copy made from an earlier one, with no first copy. We can explain any given copy of the book in terms of the previous book from which it was copied; but this will never lead us to a complete explanation, no matter how far back we go in the series of books. For we can always ask: Why have there always been such books? Why were these books written? Why were they written in the way they were? The different states of the world are like that series of books: each state is in a way copied from the preceding state – though here the "copying" isn't an exact transcription, but happens in accordance with certain laws of change. And so, with the world as with the books; however far back we might go into earlier and earlier states we'll never find in them a complete explanation for why there is any world at all, and why the world is as it is. It's not that in the backward search we'll reach a first state of the world, with no earlier one to explain it. So far as that is concerned, you are welcome to imagine that the world has always existed. But you are assuming only a succession of states, and no reason for the world can be found in any one of them (or in any set of

them, however large); so obviously the reason for the world must be found elsewhere. That means: out of the world, i.e. out of the totality of finite things, and so in something infinite and eternal. . . . From this it appears that even if we assume the past eternity of the world, we can't escape the ultimate and out-of-the-world reason for things, namely God. . . . The reasons for the world, therefore, lie hidden in something outside the world, something different from the chain of states or series of things that jointly constitute the world. And so we must move from physical or hypothetical necessity, which determines the later things in the world from the earlier to something that is absolutely or metaphysically necessary, for which a reason can't be given. (Leibniz, 1989: 149ff.)[27]

And in the *Principles of Nature and Grace, Based on Reason*, Leibniz offers further defense of the cosmological argument.

The sufficient reason for the existence of the universe cannot be found in the series of contingent things, that is, in the series of bodies and their representations in souls; for, since matter is in itself indifferent to motion and rest, and to one motion rather than another, we cannot find in matter the reason for motion, still less the reason for a particular motion. And although the present motion found in matter comes from the preceding motion, and it, in turn, comes from a preceding motion, we will not make any progress in this way, however far we go back, for the same question always remains. Thus *the sufficient reason*, which needs no other reason, must be outside this series of contingent things, and must be found in a substance which is its cause, and which is a necessary being, carrying the reason of its existence with itself. Otherwise, we would not yet have a sufficient reason where one could end the series. And this ultimate reason for things is called *God*. (Leibniz, 1989: 210ff.)

There are, no doubt, various ways to formulate the argument that Leibniz offers in these passages. Indeed, it's obvious that several arguments are offered in these passages. But, restricting attention

---

[27] Compare Leibniz (1973: secs. 36–38) and Leibniz (1996: secs. 36–37, 44–45, 49–52, 121–122).

to contingent beings, the general form of Leibniz's argument seems to be the following (Oppy, 2006: 119ff.).[28] The argument is easily generalized to contingent propositions, states of affairs, facts, events, and so on.

1. There is a maximal, finite or infinite, collection of contingent beings.
2. There is a sufficient reason for every collection of contingent beings.
3. The sufficient reason for the maximal collection of contingent beings cannot be a member of that collection.
4. Every existing being is either contingent or necessary.
5. ∴/ There is a necessary being that is the sufficient reason for the maximal collection of contingent beings.

According to Leibniz, the necessary being that is the sufficient reason for the maximal collection of contingent beings is called *God*. Leibniz (1996: sec. 7) fills out the cosmological argument with an account of the nature of God. The account aims to show that the sufficient reason for the maximal collection of contingent beings is not merely called God, but is in fact the traditional God.

> First, insofar as the first cause of the entire series must have been able to survey all other possible worlds, it has understanding. Second, insofar as it was able to select one world among the infinity of possible worlds, it has a will. Third, insofar as it was able to bring about this world, it has power. ... Fourth, insofar as the first cause relates to all possibles, its understanding, will and power are infinite. And, fifth, insofar as everything is connected together, there is no reason to suppose more than one God. Thus, Leibniz is able to *demonstrate* the uniqueness of God, his omniscience, omnipotence, and benevolence from the twin assumptions of the contingency of the world and the Principle of Sufficient Reason. (Look, 2017)

The objections that Leibniz's cosmological argument fails to show that the sufficient reason for the maximal collection of contingent

---

[28] Compare Oppy (2006).

beings is the traditional God or that the argument fails to show that there is a unique sufficient reason for the maximal collection are misplaced (Oppy, 2006: 120ff.). Leibniz takes up those topics largely in the *Theodicy* and not in either *On the Ultimate Origination of Things* or the *Principles of Nature and Grace, Based on Reason.*

The validity of the Leibnizian cosmological argument also does not appear to be a problem. The premises in (1)–(4) entail the conclusion in (5). But there are concerns about both the interpretation and truth of the propositions in (1)–(5). It is fascinating that Leibniz noticed that an infinite sequence, series, or collection of contingent beings would not undermine the cosmological argument. Premise (1) allows that the collection of contingent beings might have an infinite cardinality and premise (2) requires that the infinite collection have a sufficient reason. Leibniz urged that the same questions remain whether the collection is finite or infinite. The infinite collection itself needs a sufficient reason.

> From this it appears that even if we assume the past eternity of the world, we can't escape the ultimate and out-of-the-world reason for things, namely God. ... The reasons for the world, therefore, lie hidden in something outside the world, something different from the chain of states or series of things that jointly constitute the world. (Leibniz, 1973: 136)

But David Hume famously objected that an infinite collection of individuals, suitably related, is sufficiently explained. Here is Hume.

> Did I show you the particular causes of each individual in a collection of twenty particles of matter, I should think it very unreasonable, should you afterwards ask me, what was the cause of the whole twenty. This is sufficiently explained in explaining the cause of the parts. (Hume, 1907: 120)

And it does seem true, as Hume observes, that once every particular contingent being in a collection is explained we have an explanation for the whole collection of contingent beings.

Paul Edwards also sees a basic confusion in the request for an explanation for the collection of contingent objects.

> The demand to find the cause of the series as a whole rests on the erroneous assumption that the series is something over and above the members of which it is composed. ... Like the expression "this dog" or "this man" the phrase "this series" is easily taken to designate an individual object. But reflection shows this to be an error. (Edwards, 1967: 113)

The problem with the Hume–Edwards view is that no contingent fact – and no conjunction of contingent facts – finite or infinite can explain a maximal contingent fact or a maximal spatiotemporally related object.

Let MCCF be a maximal conjunctive contingent fact, state of affairs, or proposition. MCCF conjoins all and only contingent facts. The explanandum for MCCF, according to Hume and Edwards, is just the explananda for each conjunct of MCCF. Call that explanans $MCCF_1$. Since MCCF is contingent, we know that its explanans $MCCF_1$ is also contingent. But $MCCF_1$ is contingent only if $MCCF_1$ is conjoined in MCCF. But then $MCCF_1$ must be both contingent and self-explanatory, and that's impossible.

Of course, it might be urged that $MCCF_1$ is not self-explanatory, rather $MCCF_2$ explains $MCCF_1$. But $MCCF_2$ is also contingent and so also a conjunct of MCCF. But then $MCCF_2$ must be contingent and self-explanatory. But that's impossible. So, there must be some $MCCF_3$ that explains $MCCF_2$ and so on infinitely. But, in general, for every n, $MCCF_n$ is a contingent conjunct of MCCF. But MCCF is the explanandum, and the conjunction of all $MCCF_n$ is a contingent conjunct of MCCF, so the conjunction of all $MCCF_n$ must be contingent and self-explanatory. But that's impossible.

The sufficient reason for MCCF cannot be a contingent conjunct of MCCF. But every contingent explanation $MCCF_n$ is a contingent conjunct of MCCF. So no contingent explanation can explain MCCF. The sufficient reason for MCCF cannot be a contingent fact.

3.2 The Threat of Modal Collapse

There is no contingent explanation for a maximal contingent fact, state of affairs, or proposition. Any contingent explanation will be a conjunct in the maximal fact and therefore cannot be an explanation for the maximal fact. But there is a powerful argument that there is also no *necessary explanation* for a maximal contingent fact, state of affairs, or proposition. If there is no contingent explanation and no necessary explanation for maximal contingent facts, state of affairs, or propositions, then maximal contingent facts are necessarily brute facts and the principle of sufficient reason is false.

3.3 The Argument for Modal Collapse

The argument against the principle of sufficient reason aims to show that the largest contingent conjunction W must have a necessary explanation.[29] W has a necessary explanation, according to NE, only if W is necessarily true. NE. p necessarily explains q only if (i) p is necessarily true, (ii) p entails q, and (iii) q is necessarily true.

And, it follows from principles O and K that W is necessarily true only if W is necessarily actual.

O. $\Box$(W is true $\leftrightarrow$ W is actual)
K. $\Box(p \rightarrow q) \rightarrow (\Box p \rightarrow \Box q)$

Therefore, the argument concludes, W is a necessitarian world, or, equivalently, W is the only possible world.[30] The initial premise in the argument is that W is a true, maximal contingent conjunction.

1. W is a true, maximal contingent conjunction.

    According to the principle of sufficient reason, every true proposition has an explanation, so W has an explanation.

---

[29] Compare Dasgupta (2016), Schnieder and Steinberg (2016), Smith (1995), and Vallicella (1997).

[30] See Bennett (1984: 115), Ross (1969: 295–304), Rowe (1988: 94ff.), and van Inwagen (1983: 202–204, 2009: 150ff.), and recently in Francken and Geirsson (1999).

2. W has an explanation. From the principle of sufficient reason, (1).

   But W cannot have a contingent explanation, since every true contingent proposition is a conjunct of W. But no contingent explanation of W can be a contingent conjunct of W. Since every contingent proposition is a contingent conjunct of W, no contingent proposition can be a contingent explanation for W.

3. Necessarily, there is no contingent explanation for W. From (1).

   But it follows from the principle of sufficient reason that every true proposition has an explanation, and every explanation is either a contingent explanation or a necessary explanation.

4. For every true proposition there is either a contingent explanation of a necessary explanation. From the principle of sufficient reason.

   But then W must have a necessary explanation, since it cannot have a contingent explanation.

5. There is a necessary explanation for W. The principle of sufficient reason, (2), (3), (4).

   But it follows from NE and (5) that W is necessarily true.

6. W is necessarily true. NE, (5).

   But then it follows from the closure principle K and principle O that W is a necessitarian world.

7. W is a necessitarian world. (6), K, O.

It follows from (7) that W is characterized by total modal collapse. For every proposition p in W, p is possible if and only if p is true if and only if p is necessary. Indeed, it follows from (7) that, necessarily, all modal distinctions collapse. Modal collapse appears to be the cost of the principle of sufficient reason and absolute explanation.

Premise (1) of course states that W is contingent conjunction, and not necessarily true. If we want to preserve the contingency of W, then our only option appears to be to reject the principle of sufficient reason. Indeed, the conclusion of Peter van Inwagen and Jonathan Bennett is that the principle of sufficient reason is, unfortunately, false. We know that the principle of sufficient reason is false, according to van Inwagen and Bennett, since we know that the actual world is contingent.[31]

Section 4 Modal Realism and the Cosmological Argument

Genuine modal realism is the view that possible worlds are concrete sums of spatiotemporally related concrete parts. Possible worlds are not maximal states of affairs or properties. Possible worlds are not maximal sets of propositions. Possible worlds are not even maximal concrete facts. Possible worlds are composite concrete objects.

Possible worlds are concrete mereological sums – and not maximal states of affairs or maximal propositions – so multiple concrete possible worlds can coexist. This is not equivalent to the multiverse idea of many universes existing in a single possible world. Instead we have many concrete possible worlds coexisting. According to theistic modal realism, all possible worlds coexist. Indeed, all possible worlds *necessarily* coexist. The collection of all possible worlds is the pluriverse or the totality of metaphysical space.

The explananda of cosmological arguments is the entire concrete pluriverse. There is an absolute explanation for the pluriverse that entails that the pluriverse – the totality of metaphysical space – necessarily exists. The absolute explanation is the traditional view that God necessarily creates the totality of metaphysical space since God necessarily manifests divine glory in creating everything.[32] The absolute explanation entails that all possible

---

[31] A referee notes that actualist views that reject absolute explanation of course avoid modal collapse. That's true, but as we have noted earlier, absolute explanations really do explain everything, and it would be great to combine absolute explanations and a problem-free metaphysics.

[32] A referee asks about issues related to the value of the pluriverse. First, since the pluriverse necessarily and eternally exists, every instance of evil in every world is justified evil. This is true even on the assumption that the pluriverse is plenitudinous (as I assume). God's value is, on the account I defend, absolutely infinite, beyond all cardinal measure. Since God exists in the pluriverse (from the standpoint of each world, though not in any particular world), the value of

worlds are necessarily existing concrete objects and so the actual world – and of course everything it contains – is a necessarily existing concrete object.

The actual world is a necessarily existing concrete object, but that does not entail that the actual world is the only possible world. Genuine modal realism – more precisely, theistic modal realism – does not generate the problem of modal fatalism. Theistic modal realism affords the most powerful cosmological argument available, since it permits an absolute explanation for everything – an explanation for the entire pluriverse – without entailing modal fatalism or generating the problem of causal indeterminism, the problem of contingency, the problem of libertarian freedom, or the problem of lawless worlds.

4.1 Necessitarianism and Contingency

As Hud Hudson observed, many have taken the necessitarian conclusion as a decisive objection to the principle of sufficient reason and therefore to the Leibnizian cosmological argument.

> Unfortunately for the rationalists, however, it would appear that the principle of sufficient reason has recently been shown to have an incredible consequence, namely, that every truth is a logically necessary truth. Few rationalists are willing to pay that price for their principle, and the thesis that there exist brute facts is now more popular among metaphysicians than ever before. (Hudson, 1997: 77)

Some have aimed to weaken the principle of sufficient reason in order to accommodate libertarian free choice and quantum indeterminism (Pruss, 2012: 56–57).[33] On this view, it is a sufficient explanation of libertarian free action – not, certainly, the best sort

---

the pluriverse too is absolutely infinite. I'm not sure how to answer counterpossibles such as "what value would the pluriverse have had had God not created it?" since the evaluation of counterpossibles is too controversial. These points are taken up in detail in Almeida (2017a, 2017b), and in *Theism and Modal Realism* (unpublished).

[33] See also Pruss (2006: chs. 7–8).

of explanation – that an agent had non-determining reasons S to perform some action A and non-determining reasons T to perform B, and the agent happened to be impressed by S rather than T. The result, of course, is that by the standards of the best explanations, the weaker explanation requires the acceptance of a host of brute facts. The best sort of explanation does not allow, most obviously, that the agent happened to be impressed by S rather than T in w, and happened to be impressed by T rather than S in w'.

But there is a way to reconcile necessitarianism, contingency, and indeterminism without permitting any brute facts at all. There is, indeed, also a way to reconcile necessitarianism and lawless worlds without permitting any brute facts. Theistic modal realism offers the promised reconciliation without compromising on the principle of sufficient reason. But theistic modal realism does require a commitment to what some see as an ontologically extravagant picture of metaphysical reality. Theistic modal realism envisages the totality of metaphysical reality as a vast concrete pluriverse.

Familiar forms of actualist realism, though ontologically less extravagant, have the peculiar implication that either all possible worlds – including the actual world – are abstract objects or that the actual "world" is not a possible world at all.

> There is also the option of reducing possible worlds to maximal consistent "books" of propositions. ... But is this reductive option credible? I find it absolutely incredible that our actual world is a maximal consistent book of propositions! (Lewis, 2015: 19–20)

The alternative is to maintain the reduction of worlds to books but declare that the actual world is not a possible world. That consequence is also untenable. For theistic modal realists – for genuine modal realists generally – possible worlds are not understood as maximally consistent sets of propositions or as maximally consistent states of affairs or as maximal properties or the like. Possible worlds are not abstract objects that might be concretized. Possible worlds are instead causally and spatiotemporally closed or isolated individuals. A possible world just is the totality of spatiotemporally related parts.

Theistic modal realism rejects the thesis that the actual world and its contents comprise the totality of metaphysical reality. There is much more to metaphysical reality than what we find in actuality. Possible worlds – including the actual world – are just particular concrete regions of the much larger concrete pluriverse. Actuality is just the region of metaphysical reality that we happen to inhabit (Lewis, 1973: 86ff.).

What exists, in the most inclusive and least restrictive sense, is the concrete pluriverse and all of its inhabitants. Everything that exists in the absolutely unrestricted sense *necessarily* exists. From the point of view of every possible world the very same things exist unrestrictedly. Indeed the pluriverse itself exists necessarily. Nothing could have been any different from the way it is, if we understand "reality" unrestrictedly as the entire pluriverse – literally all of metaphysical reality. There are no grander and grander pluralities (Skyrms, 1976), no alternative pluralities, no other way the pluriverse might have been. The totality of metaphysical reality exists necessarily.

Theistic modal realism takes as the object of God's creation the totality of metaphysical reality. In direct contrast to theistic actualist realism, theistic modal realism makes it possible that God creates more than one possible world. Indeed, theistic modal realism maintains that God necessarily creates every possible world, the entire pluriverse, and everything in the pluriverse.

The totality of metaphysical reality is the object of God's creation. All possibilia exist in exactly the same way that all actualia exist. Possibilia do not exist vicariously via proxies – individual essences or suitable qualitative descriptions – in the actual world. Nor do possibilia exist as contingently non-concrete objects. And possible worlds do not exist as uninstantiated maximal sets of sentences or the like. Rather, all possible worlds and possibilia exist as parts of the concrete totality of metaphysical reality. Unicorns exist not as concepts in the mind of God or abstract objects, but as concrete objects in the pluriverse, and similarly for talking donkeys, flying pigs, and all other possible objects. To the question what did God create, the answer is absolutely unrestrictedly everything! What exists could not be more plenitudinous than divine creation is – the glory of God is necessarily manifested in the vast creation of the pluriverse.

But how does theistic modal realism reconcile necessitarianism, contingency, and indeterminism? Peter van Inwagen, Jonathan Bennett, and William Rowe argue that there is an absolute explanation for the actual world only if there are no contingent facts. The argument, as we saw, is that there is an absolute explanation for the actual world – an explanation for why our particular world is actual and not some other possible world – only if the actual world obtains as a matter of metaphysical necessity. The absolute explanation entails that there are then no contingent facts, and all modal distinctions collapse. Here is van Inwagen.

> Someone might suggest, for example, that the actual future became actual not for any reason to be found in the natural world but rather because God chose that it should, God's choice being in that case the sufficient reason. ... However, PSR must be rejected, for it has an absurd consequence: the collapse of all modal distinctions. (van Inwagen, 1983: 202–204)[34]

But what's sometimes called "the paradox of sufficient reason" is not a problem for theistic modal realism (Levey, 2016). On theistic modal realism, the object of God's creation is the entire pluriverse, not merely our particular region of it. The principle of sufficient reason requires an absolute explanation and therefore entails that the *pluriverse as a whole, and everything in it, exists as a matter of metaphysical necessity*. It is the pluriverse and everything in it that fully satisfies the principle of sufficient reason. There is a necessarily true proposition – the proposition that God necessarily manifests his glory in the creation of the pluriverse – that entails (and so explains) the existence of the pluriverse and everything in the pluriverse. Of course it is also true that *the actual world and everything in it necessarily exists*, since the actual world is one region of a necessarily existing pluriverse.

---

[34] See also van Inwagen (2009: 150ff.).

Given that the pluriverse exists necessarily and that, therefore, the actual world exists necessarily, and further given that everything in the pluriverse has all of its properties essentially, how *could* theistic modal realism preserve contingency? There simply seems no room for contingency in the pluriverse at all and that seems to be the problem that van Inwagen and others are so worried about.

On theistic modal realism, every world is necessarily the way that it is, but this is consistent with contingency in the pluriverse. The Earth, to take an example of one part of our world, is necessarily as it is in the sense that nothing meeting the strictest or most rigorous standards of similarity to the Earth could fail to have any of its actual properties. Nothing meeting the strictest standards of similarity to the Earth could fail to have even its most minor and insignificant properties. When the standards of similarity are high – when we are speaking in the strict and philosophical sense – nothing in the pluriverse counts as being the Earth except the Earth.

Nonetheless, we can truthfully say that it is a contingent fact that the Earth is inhabited. We can truthfully say that it is a contingent fact that the earth is inhabited because we are prepared to accept lower standards of similarity according to which an uninhabited Earth – a strictly nonidentical counterpart of the Earth – in some region of metaphysical space counts as being the Earth in that region.

Varying standards on similarity feature prominently in discussions of just what is possible and what is not. Most of us are willing to accommodate various standards in ordinary discussion. By some standards Babe Ruth could have been a ballerina. By other standards he couldn't have been. By some standards, to borrow an example from David Lewis, I can speak Finnish; by other standards I cannot. By the strictest standards on similarity, I certainly cannot.

All contingency arises from the accommodation of assertions that presuppose less than perfectly strict standards of similarity in the selection of counterparts. Our counterparts are our representatives or just those beings in metaphysical space that count as being us under some standard of similarity. Could Hubert Humphrey have been a poached egg? According to some very loose standard of similarity, poached eggs exist in some regions of the pluriverse that count as being Humphrey. You accept that Humphrey might have been a poached egg only if you are prepared to accept such loose standards. But you don't have to accept those standards – and most folks are just not *that* accommodating. Could Socrates have been an alligator? Plantinga, for one, seems to think the answer is yes (Plantinga, 1974a).

If you resist any standard of similarity according to which a poached egg exists that counts as being Hubert Humphrey, then you deny Humphrey might have been a poached egg. As a matter of empirical fact we are very accommodating in this way, and you might be prepared to accept standards according to which Humphrey could have been a clever talking donkey or an intelligent alligator or born to Egyptian parents or a robot (Lewis, 1986: 251ff.). With sufficiently low standards on similarity, there's a vast amount of contingency in the world. Those low standards are indeed what make contingent statements true.[35]

Having an absolute explanation does entail that the totality of metaphysical reality – including our region of metaphysical reality and everything in our region of metaphysical reality – is necessarily as it is. In the strict and philosophical sense, nothing could be even slightly different from the way it is. But absolute explanations do not entail that there is no contingency in the pluriverse. Contingency arises in the pluriverse – as it does for any view on the nature of metaphysical reality – from lowering the standards on representation. It is because of the accommodation of low standards permitting less and less similar items in the pluriverse to count as being, say, the RMS *Queen Mary*, that we agree that it might have been longer or shorter or faster or a skyscraper or an

---

[35] For further references to this phenomenon, see Lewis (1979, 1986). Many thanks to Mark Johnston and Wolfgang Schwarz for valuable discussion of these points.

airplane and so on. And it is true to say on those standards that the RMS *Queen Mary* might have been slower and so on. But on the strictest standards of similarity, the RMS *Queen Mary* could not have been any of those things, since on those standards the RMS *Queen Mary* has all of its properties essentially. On the strictest standards, only the RMS *Queen Mary* is a counterpart of the RMS *Queen Mary*.

As we noted earlier, the paradox of sufficient reason is not a problem for theistic modal realism. The principle of sufficient reason entails that there is an absolute explanation for the pluriverse. For theistic modal realists, the *pluriverse as a whole, and everything in it, exists as a matter of metaphysical necessity.* It is the pluriverse and everything in it that fully satisfies the principle of sufficient reason. There is a necessarily true proposition – the proposition that God necessarily manifests his glory in the creation of the pluriverse – that entails the existence of the pluriverse and everything in the pluriverse. Of course it is also true that *the actual world and everything in it also necessarily exist,* since the actual world is one region of a necessarily existing pluriverse. But there is also a vast amount of contingency in the pluriverse. Virtually everything in the pluriverse could have been different in countless ways.

4.2 Indeterminism and Libertarianism

Free will libertarians maintain that free will is incompatible with determinism. They've argued that, since the principle of sufficient reason entails necessitarianism, and since necessitarianism entails that no one could do anything other than they in fact do, the principle of sufficient reason is incompatible with libertarian free will.

> The basic intuition of a libertarian is that determinism places the ultimate point of decision outside the agent, in the environment that forms and influences the agent. This external determinism, to produce freedom, must not only be removed but must be replaced by something causal, though still indeterministic in the case of agents that have a cause of their existence, within the agent. (Pruss, 2012: 55)

The argument for necessitarianism shows that the totality of metaphysical reality is necessarily as it is. So, every region of the pluriverse, and every part of every region, is also necessarily as it is. But if the actual world is necessarily as it is – if every event that occurs, state of affairs that obtains, every object that exists, necessarily occurs, obtains, and exists – then there appears to be no room for indeterminism or libertarian free choice.

Theistic modal realism makes indeterminism compatible with necessitarianism. We'll say that an event A is undetermined in possible world w if there is another possible world w' and time t such that w and w' are exactly the same up to t, but that A occurs at t in w and ~A occurs at t in w'. Possible worlds do not overlap at all with respect to individuals, so w and w' do not branch from a common past. We'll say instead that the past in w' up to t duplicates the past in w up to t, and w and w' diverge at time t. Duplicates are intrinsically indiscernible, but they are not identical. There are two pasts – the past of w and the past of w' – but the two pasts are intrinsically the same. The laws of nature in w and w' are exactly the same, but the conjunction of all laws in w, L, and the history of w up to t, H, do not together determine that A occurs at t. This is because there is a world w' that duplicates w up to t, H', and includes L, but where ~A occurs at t.

Once again we are all prepared to accommodate the assertion that ~A might have occurred at t given the sorts of laws we have in w. Our accommodation involves accepting a weaker standard of similarity according to which H' counts as being H. Under the weaker standard of similarity we allow some flexibility in what it is to be H and maintain that $\sim\Box((H \& L) \rightarrow A)$, and truthfully say that w is not a deterministic world.

4.3 Necessitarianism and Lawless Worlds

Laws of nature – causal laws – are at least exceptionless regularities, and we may say something similar about stochastic or probabilistic laws. If it is a causal law that it is probable that B's follows on A's, there should be no exceptions to that stochastic relationship. We should not find, for instance, that the stochastic relationship between A's and B's fluctuates over time, or that there is no regular stochastic relationship at all between A's and B's. The objection from lawless worlds is an argument from the contingency of causal laws. There are in the pluriverse possible worlds in which there are no causal laws at all. Possible worlds with no causal laws do not admit of the causal explanation of the existence of any object, occurrence of any event, or obtaining of any fact. That is not consistent with the absolute explanation of the pluriverse.

It is of course perfectly possible that worlds in the pluriverse lack all regularity relationships among events, facts, propositions, or whatever we take to be the relata of causation. It might be false for all A and B that there are any universal or stochastic causal laws relating them. In worlds without any causal laws, every event that occurs and every fact that obtains does so *uncaused*. It is true in such worlds that there is no causal explanation for anything that exists, occurs, or obtains. Principles of causation are false in such worlds. The general principle of causation states that necessarily, for every fact, event, or object there is some cause. It is the denial of the thesis that possibly, some objects rather come into existence *causelessly ex nihilo*. The general causal principle requires some causal explanation for each particular fact, event, and object. But of course in lawless worlds there is no causal explanation for any fact, event, or object.

In lawless worlds the occurrences of events, the existence of objects, and the obtaining of facts are not governed by causal laws. The appearances of causal relations in the world and the appearances of causal regularities in nature are entirely illusory. We should add that, for all we know, for all our observational evidence assures us, our world is a lawless world in which the appearance of regularities in nature is an illusion. Our regularities might be no more than quasi-regularities and our laws might be no more than quasi-laws.

The argument for necessitarianism shows that the totality of metaphysical reality is necessarily as it is. So, every region of the pluriverse, and every part of every region, is also necessarily as it is. Our world is a hyper-essential world. Everything has all of its properties essentially. But if every event that occurs, state of affairs that obtains, every object that exists, necessarily occurs, obtains, and exists, then how could there be lawless worlds in the pluriverse? How could there be lawless worlds given the absolute explanation of everything in the pluriverse?

It is possible that no event occurs or fact obtains according to any causal laws – universal or stochastic – in world w, and that everything in w occurs or obtains necessarily as it does.[36] Everything in a causally patternless world occurs, obtains, or exists necessarily. There are several important consequences. First, divine providence is perfectly possible in lawless worlds in which everything exists necessarily. Second, the falsity of the principle of causation presents no problem for the cosmological argument. The truth of the principle of sufficient reason is compatible with the falsity of the principle of causality. There must be an explanation for causally lawless worlds just as there must be an explanation of causally lawful worlds. Third, the necessitarian conclusion of the Bennett–van Inwagen argument presents no obstacle to the existence of lawless worlds. Necessitarianism is consistent not only with contingency and indeterminism but also with causal lawlessness.

4.4 Necessitarianism and Modal Imagination

The problem of modal imagination is sometimes called the Humean problem for the principle of sufficient reason.

> One can, arguably, imagine that a brick pops into existence uncaused. Therefore, one might conclude that it is possible that a brick pops into existence uncaused, and hence that the PSR is not a necessary truth. This is a popular Humean argument against the PSR. (Pruss, 2012: 47)

---

[36] In the worlds I'm describing, there are *no exceptionless regularities*. Laws, whatever else they turn out to be, are at least exceptionless regularities. That's just a necessary condition on something's being a (physical) law. Since there are (at least small) exceptions to every rule that might govern nature in the world I describe, those rules are not laws. They are not laws even if they turn out to be necessary.

John Mackie defends the Humean argument from modal imagination.

> As Hume pointed out, we can certainly conceive an uncaused beginning-to-be of an object: if what we can thus conceive is nevertheless in some way impossible, this still requires to be shown. (Mackie, 1983: 89)[37]

Further on Mackie writes:

> [T]here is a priori no good reason why a sheer origination of things, not determined by anything, should be unacceptable, whereas the existence of god with the power to create something out of nothing is acceptable. (Mackie, 1983: 94)

The Humean argues that there is no conceptual impossibility in any object simply "popping into" into existence uncaused. Craig complains that the Humean argument entails that there are chaotic worlds in which unlimited numbers and kinds of objects simply come into existence *ex nihilo*.

> Does Mackie sincerely believe that things can pop into existence uncaused, out of nothing? Does anyone in his right mind believe that, say, a raging tiger could suddenly come into existence uncaused, out of nothing, in this room right now? The same applies to the universe: if prior to the universe there was absolutely nothing – no God, no space, no time – how could the universe possibly have come to exist? (Craig, 1998: 25)

Jonathan Edwards argues similarly that if we perhaps allow some things – say, volitions – to come into existence uncaused, then we must allow that anything can come into existence uncaused.

> It is ... as repugnant to reason, to suppose that an act of the will should come into existence without a cause, as to suppose the human soul, or an angel, or the globe of the earth, or the whole universe, should come into existence without a cause. And if once

---

[37] See also Hume (1981, Book I, Part iii, Section II). But compare Anscombe (1974) and Craig (1984).

we allow, that such a sort of effect as a Volition may come to pass without a Cause, how do we know but that many other sorts of effects may do so too? (Edwards, 2003: 15ff.)

As with the objection from the contingency of laws – the argument that lawless possible worlds exist – theistic modal realism can easily manage the objection from the imaginability of chaotic worlds. Chaotic worlds are consistent with the absolute explanation of the pluriverse and every world in the pluriverse.

Timothy Williamson observed that necessitism does not entail permanentism. Necessitism is the view that everything that exists, necessarily exists. More precisely, it is the view that necessarily everything that exists necessarily exists. But the fact that every object exists necessarily does not entail that every object is permanent or that the sequence of events in a world is predicable or causally intelligible. Necessarily existing objects may go out of existence and come into existence on a regular or irregular schedule.

Let's say that a possible world is hyper-essentialist just in case every property of every object is an essential property. Necessitism does not entail hyper-essentiality. Necessarily existing objects might gain and lose properties in the same way that contingently existing properties gain and lose properties.

Absolute explanation entails necessitism and hyper-essentiality. Since there is an absolute explanation for everything in the pluriverse, everything in the pluriverse exists necessarily and everything has all of its properties essentially. But the fact that there is an absolute explanation of the pluriverse does not entail that there are no chaotic worlds. Chaotic worlds are just those that concern Edwards and Craig. These are possible worlds in which various kinds of objects, events, and states of affairs come into existence and go out of existence with no causal explanation. But we know that there are possible worlds in which no causal regularities obtain and no causal laws are true. In possible worlds where there are no true causal laws, there are no true causal explanations. But it is not true that there are no explanations at all in such worlds.

Imagine an oscillating world in which there are no exceptionless regularities. Instead, in every even epoch, universal generalizations of the form all A's follow B's are true. In every odd epoch, stochastic generalizations of the form 85 percent of all A's follow B's. In oscillating worlds we have no causal explanations for anything that comes into existence, but we do have epoch relative explanations. But these oscillating worlds are not of course chaotic worlds.

Imagine an oscillating chaotic world in which there are no exceptionless regularities. Instead, in every even minute the world is governed by true stochastic generalizations of the form 2n ($1 < n < 50$) percent of all A's are B's are true. In every odd minute the world is governed by true stochastic generalizations of the form (2n – 1) ($1 < n < 50$) percent of all A's are B's are true. The oscillating chaotic world has no causal laws at all. Indeed, there is vast variation in stochastic generalizations governing the world; from minute to minute there are different governing generalizations. Objects are coming into existence and going out of existence in unpredictable ways and events are occurring minute to minute in ways that cannot be predicted.

As the Humean objection goes, such chaotic worlds are conceivable. And indeed as Mackie suggests, the conceivability of such worlds is good evidence for the possibility of such worlds. But such worlds are perfectly compatible with every chaotic event occurring as a matter of necessity. It is not difficult to imagine a Spinozistic chaotic world in which the temporal unfolding events, objects, and states of affairs could not have been otherwise, despite the fact that the occurrence of events, the existence of objects, and the obtaining of states of affairs is radically unpredictable. The radical unpredictability of a world is perfectly consistent with the fact that a world is necessitated. So, the fact that a world has an absolute explanation does not entail that the world is not radically unpredictable.

It interesting to note that the fact that a world is radically unpredictable does not entail that the world is *unintelligible.* The chaotic world described is intelligible since, for every event that occurs in the world, the event occurs as a matter of metaphysical necessity and for every object that exists in the world, the object exists as a matter of metaphysical necessity. Everything in the world has an absolute explanation.

In oscillating chaotic worlds objects are coming into existence both unpredictably and uncaused, since there are no causal laws. But just as in lawless worlds and in oscillating non-chaotic worlds, there is a local non-causal explanation for why objects come into existence and go out of existence. The local explanations in chaotic worlds are relative to time-sensitive stochastic generalizations. The explanations at time t for the objects of type x coming into existence will differ from explanations at time t' for objects of type x coming into existence. None of these local explanations will be causal explanations.

The existence of chaotic worlds in the pluriverse is not a problem for theistic modal realism. According to theistic modal realism there is an absolute explanation for the pluriverse and everything in the pluriverse. As a matter of metaphysical necessity, the pluriverse could not be any different from the way that it is, and so as a matter of metaphysical necessity every possible world, and every part of every possible world, could not be any different from the way that it is. But there are chaotic worlds in the pluriverse, worlds in which the occurrence of events, the existence of objects, and the obtaining of states of affairs is radically unpredictable. Could a raging tiger suddenly come into existence in the room, or could a brick simply pop into existence uncaused?

The answer to those questions is yes. But we really should observe, first, that these events are not as foreign or incomprehensible as Craig, Pruss, Edwards, and others suggest. Indeed, events of the very same kind are not ruled out in our own world. If you drop a plate, for instance, there is a small chance that the particles composing the plate fly off sideways and the plate does not hit the floor (Hawthorne, 2006). There is some small chance, further, that the particles that compose the hand of the statue of David all move together upward and then downward and "wave" at you (Dawkins, 1996). Or consider the unlikely quantum event that a marble I drop tunnels through the whole house and lands on the ground underneath, leaving the matter it penetrates intact (Lasonen-Aarnio and Hawthorne, 2010). Or consider that, for any actual object whatsoever, there is a small chance that it spontaneously disappears and an intrinsic duplicate of the object appears on Mars (Williams, 2008). All of these events have some small chance of actually happening. In chaotic worlds such events happen often and unpredictably. But many of the events in chaotic worlds are not radically different in kind from events that can actually occur.

Contingency, necessitarianism, lawlessness, modal imagination, and indeterminism are all reconciled on theistic modal realism. There is no serious ontological cost imposed by absolute explanations or the principle of sufficient reason. There is no paradox of sufficient reason for modal realists. Necessitarianism is true, on this account, since unrestrictedly everything is necessarily as it is. The actual world, in particular, and everything in the actual world, is necessarily as it is. Contingency and indeterminism are preserved given the comparatively low standards we are all prepared to accept on representation. Given sufficiently low standards Caesar might not have crossed the Rubicon and I might throw a stone faster than the speed of light. And the possibility of lawlessness is preserved since causally patternless worlds might include events, objects, and facts that necessarily occur, exist, and obtain.

References

Adams, Robert M. (1974) "Theories of Actuality," *Noûs* 8: 211–231.

(1981) "Actualism and Thisness," *Synthese* 49: 3–41.

Alexander, H. G. (1956) *The Leibniz–Clarke Correspondence*. Oxford: University of Manchester Press.

Al-Ghazali (1962) *Kitab al-Iqtisad fi 'l-Iqtiqad*. Ankara: University of Ankara Press.

(1963) *Tahafut al-Falasifah*. Lahore: Pakistan Philosophical Congress.

Almeida, Michael (2008) *The Metaphysics of Perfect Beings*. London: Routledge.

(2010) "O'Connor's Permissive Multiverse," *Philosophia Christi* 12: 297–308.

(2011) "Theistic Modal Realism?," in Jonathan L. Kvanvig (ed.), *Oxford Studies in Philosophy of Religion*. Volume 3. Oxford: Oxford University Press. 1–15.

(2017a) "Theistic Modal Realism I: The Challenge of Actualist Realism," *Philosophy Compass* 12 (2017): 1–14.

(2017b) "Theistic Modal Realism II: Theoretical Benefits," *Philosophy Compass* 12 (2017): 1–17.

Anscombe, G. E. M. (1974) "'Whatever Has a Beginning of Existence Must Have a Cause': Hume's Argument Exposed," *Analysis* 34 (5): 145–151.

Aquinas, St. Thomas (1263a) *Summa Contra Gentiles Book I: God*, Anton C. Pegis, F.R.S.C. (trans.). South Bend, IN: University of Notre Dame Press, 1979.

(1263b) *Summa Contra Gentiles Book II: Creation*, James F. Anderson (trans.). South Bend, IN: University of Notre Dame Press, 1979.

(1271) "On the Eternity of the World," in Ralph McInerny (ed.), *Thomas Aquinas: Selected Writings*. London: Penguin Books, 1998. 710–717.

(1273) *Summa Theologica*. Volume I. Scotts Valley, CA: Nov Antique Publishers, 2008.

Benacerraf, Paul (1962) "Tasks, Super-Tasks and the Modern Eleatics," *Journal of Philosophy* LIX (24): 765–768.

Benardete, José (1964) *Infinity: An Essay in Metaphysics.* Oxford: Clarendon Press.

Bennett, Jonathan (1984) *A Study of Spinoza's Ethics.* Indianapolis, IN: Hackett Publishing.

Bird, Alexander (2005) "The Dispositionalist Conception of Laws," *Foundations of Science* 10: 353–370.

(2007) *Nature's Metaphysics: Laws and Properties.* Oxford: Oxford University Press.

Bonaventure, ca. 1250, *Commentary on the Sentences: Philosophy of God. Works of St. Bonaventure,* vol. XVI, R. E. Houser and Timothy B. Noone (eds.), St. Bonaventure, NY: Franciscan Institute Press, 2014.

Burrill, Donald R. (1967) *The Cosmological Argument.* New York, NY: Anchor Books.

Cantor, Georg (1915) *Contributions to the Founding of the Theory of Transfinite Numbers,* P. E. B. Jourdain (trans.). New York, NY: Dover Publishers.

Chalmers, David (2000) "Does Conceivability Entail Possibility?," in Tamar S. Gendler and John Hawthorne (eds.), *Conceivability and Possibility.* Oxford: Oxford University Press. 145–200.

Chisholm, Roderick (1976) *Persons and Objects.* La Salle, IL: Open Court Press.

Clarke, Samuel (1998) *A Demonstration of the Being and Attributes of God,* Ezio Vailati (ed.), Cambridge: Cambridge University Press.

Cohoe, Caleb (2013) "There Must Be a First: Why Thomas Aquinas Rejects Infinite, Essentially Ordered, Causal Series," *British Journal for the History of Philosophy* 21 (5): 838–856.

Contessa, Gabriele (2010) "Modal Truthmakers and Two Varieties of Actualism," *Synthese* 174: 341–353.

Corry, Richard (2011) "Can Dispositionalist Essences Ground the Laws of Nature?," *Australasian Journal of Philosophy* 89 (2): 263–275.

Coughlan, M. J. (1987) "Must God Create Only the Best Possible World?," *Sophia* 26: 15–19.

Craig, William Lane (1979) *The Kalām Cosmological Argument.* Eugene, OR: Wipf and Stock Publishers.

(1984) "Professor Mackie and the Kalām Cosmological Argument," *Religious Studies* 20 (3): 367–375.

(1998) "The Kalām Cosmological Argument," in Louis Pojman (ed.), *Philosophy of Religion: An Anthology.* Boston, MA: Wadsworth Publishing.24–41.

(2001) *The Cosmological Argument: From Plato to Leibniz*, Eugene, OR: Wipf and Stock Publishers.

(2016) *Reasonable Faith*. www.reasonablefaith.org/Free-Will.

Craig, William Lane and Moreland, J. P. (2015) "The Kalam Cosmological Argument," in Michael Rea and Louis Pojman (eds.), *Philosophy of Religion: An Anthology*. Stamford, CA: Cengage Publishers.

Craig, William Lane and Sinclair, James D. (2012) "The Kalam Cosmological Argument," in William Lane Craig and J. P. Moreland (eds.), *The Blackwell Companion to Natural Theology*. Oxford: Blackwell. 101–201.

Craig, William Lane and Smith, Quentin (1993) *Theism, Atheism, and Big Bang Cosmology*. Oxford: Clarendon Press.

Dasgupta, Shamik (2016) "Metaphysical Rationalism," *Noûs* 50 (2): 379–418.

Dawkins, Richard (1996) *The Blind Watchmaker*. New York, NY: W. W. Norton & Company.

Deasy, Daniel (2015) "The Moving Spotlight Theory," *Philosophical Studies* 172 (8). 2073–2089.

Della Rocca, Michael (2010) "PSR," *Philosophers Imprint* 10 (7): 1–13.

Divers, John (1999) "A Genuine Realist Theory of Advanced Modalizing," *Mind* 108: 217–239.

(2007) "The Modal Metaphysics of Alvin Plantinga," in Deane-Peter Baker (ed.), *Alvin Plantinga*. Cambridge: Cambridge University Press. 71–92.

Dorr, Cian. "Diamonds Are Forever" (unpublished manuscript).

Draper, Paul (2004) "Cosmic Fine-Tuning and Terrestrial Suffering: Parallel Problems for Naturalism and Theism," *American Philosophical Quarterly* 41: 311–321.

Edwards, Jonathan (2003) "On the Freedom of the Will," in Patrick Alexander (ed.), *The Works of Jonathan Edwards*. Volume 1. Peabody, MA: Hendrickson Publishers.

Edwards, Paul (1967) "The Cosmological Argument," in Donald R. Burrill (ed.), *The Cosmological Arguments: A Spectrum of Opinion*. New York, NY: Doubleday Anchor Books. 101–124.

Eells, Ellery (1988) "Quentin Smith on Infinity and the Past," *Philosophy of Science* 55 (3): 453–455.

Feit, Neil (1998) "More on Brute Facts," *Australasian Journal of Philosophy* 76 (4): 625–630.

Forrest, Peter (1981) "The Problem of Evil: Two Neglected Defenses," *Sophia* 20: 49–54.

(1996) *God without the Supernatural.* Ithaca, NY: Cornell University Press.

Francken, P. and Geirsson, H. (1999) "Regresses, Sufficient Reasons, and Cosmological Arguments," *Journal of Philosophical Research* 24: 285–304.

Gamow, George (1946) *One, Two, Three, Infinity.* London: Macmillan.

Griffin, Michael V. (2013) *Leibniz, God, and Necessity.* Cambridge: Cambridge University Press.

Goldschmidt, Tyron (ed.) (2013) *The Puzzle of Existence: Why Is There Something Rather than Nothing?* New York, NY: Routledge.

Grünbaum, Adolf (1991) "Creation as a Pseudo-Explanation in Current Physical Cosmology," *Erkenntnis* 35 (1–3): 233–254.

Hackett, Stuart (1957) *The Resurrection of Theism.* Chicago, IL: Moody Press.

Hawthorne, John (2000) "Before-Effect and Zeno Causality," *Noûs* 34 (4): 622–633.

(2006) "Chance and Counterfactuals," in his *Metaphysical Essays.* Oxford: Oxford University Press. 225–264.

Hilbert, David (1964) "On the Infinite," in P. Benacerraf and H. Putnam (eds.), *Philosophy of Mathematics*, Englewood Cliffs, NJ: Prentice-Hall Publishers. 183–201.

Hoefer, Carl (2016) "Causal Determinism," *The Stanford Encyclopedia of Philosophy* (Spring 2016 Edition), Edward N. Zalta (ed.), https://plato.stanford.edu/archives/spr2016/entries/determinism-causal/.

Hudson, Hud (1997) "Brute Facts," *Australasian Journal of Philosophy* 75 (1): 77–82.

(2006) *The Metaphysics of Hyperspace.* Oxford: Oxford University Press.

Hughes, G. E. and Cresswell, M. J. (1998) *A New Introduction to Modal Logic.* London: Routledge.

Hume, David (1779) *Dialogues Concerning Natural Religion.* Edinburgh: Blackwood and Sons, 1907.

(1738) *Treatise of Human Nature*, L. A. Selby-Bigge (ed.), Oxford: Oxford University Press, 1981.

(1748) *An Enquiry Concerning Human Understanding.* London. Reprinted Indianapolis, IN: Hackett Publishing, 1993.

Jager, Thomas (1982), "An Actualist Semantics for Quantified Modal Logic," *Notre Dame Journal of Formal Logic* 23 (3): 335–349.

Kaplan, David (1979) "On the Logic of Demonstratives," *Journal of Philosophical Logic* 8 (1): 81–98.

Kenny, Anthony (1969) *The Five Ways*. New York, NY: Schocken Books.

Koons, Robert (1997) "A New Look at the Cosmological Argument," *American Philosophical Quarterly* 34 (2): 193–211.

(2008) "Epistemological Foundations for the Cosmological Argument," in Jonathan L. Kvanvig (ed.), *Oxford Studies in the Philosophy of Religion*. Oxford: Oxford University Press.105–133.

(2014) "A New Kalam Argument: Revenge of the Grim Reaper," *Noûs* 48 (2): 256–267.

Kraay, Klaas (2010) "Theism, Possible Worlds, and the Multiverse," *Philosophical Studies* 47 (3): 355–368.

(2011) "Theism and Modal Collapse," *American Philosophical Quarterly* 48: 361–72

Kretzmann, Norman (2001a) *The Metaphysics of Creation*. Oxford: Oxford University Press.

(2001b) *The Metaphysics of Theism*. Oxford: Oxford University Press.

Kripke, Saul (1980) *Naming and Necessity*. Harvard, MA: Harvard University Press.

Lasonen-Aarnio, Maria and Hawthorne, John (2010) "Knowledge and Objective Chance," in Patrick Greenough and Duncan Pritchard (eds.), *Williamson on Knowledge*. Oxford: Oxford University Press. 92–108.

Leibniz, Gottfried (1697) *On the Ultimate Origination of Things*, in R. Ariew and D. Garber (eds.), *G. W. Leibniz: Philosophical Essays*. Indianapolis, IN: Hackett Publishing, 1989a. 149–154.

(1710) *Theodicy*. La Salle, IL: Open Court Press, 1996.

(1714) *Monadology*, in G. H. R. Parkinson (ed.), *Leibniz: Philosophical Writings*. Lanham, MD: Rowman and Littlefield, 1973.

(1714) *Principles of Nature and Grace, Based on Reason*, in R. Ariew and D. Garber (eds.), *G. W. Leibniz: Philosophical Essays*. Indianapolis, IN: Hackett Publishing, 1989b. 206–212.

Levey, Samuel (2016) "The Paradox of Sufficient Reason," *Philosophical Review* 125 (3): 397–430.

Lewis, David (1973) *Counterfactuals*. Oxford: Blackwell.

(1976) "The Paradoxes of Time Travel," *American Philosophical Quarterly* 3 (2)145–152.

(1979) "Scorekeeping in a Language Game," *Journal of Philosophical Logic* 8 (3): 339–359.

(1983a) *Philosophical Papers I*. Oxford: Oxford University Press.

(1983b) "Postscripts to Anselm and Actuality," in his *Philosophical Papers I*. Oxford: Oxford University Press.

(1986a) *On the Plurality of Worlds*. Oxford: Blackwell.

(1986b) *Philosophical Papers II*. Oxford: Oxford University Press.

(2015) "A Reply to Dana Scott: 'Is There Life on Possible Worlds?'" in Barry Loewer and Jonathan Schaffer (eds.), *A Companion to David Lewis*. Oxford: Wiley-Blackwell. 18–22.

Linsky, Bernard and Zalta, Edward (1994) "In Defense of the Simplest Quantified Modal Logic," James Tomberlin (ed.), *Philosophical Perspectives 8: Logic and Language*. Atascadero, CA: Ridgeview Press. 431–448.

Look, Brandon C. (2017) "Gottfried Wilhelm Leibniz," *The Stanford Encyclopedia of Philosophy*, Edward N. Zalta (ed.), https://plato.stanford.edu/archives/sum2017/entries/leibniz/.

Mackie, John L. (1955) "Evil and Omnipotence," *Mind* 64: 200–212.

(1983) *The Miracle of Theism*. Oxford: Oxford University Press.

McHarry, D. (1978) "A Theodicy," *Analysis*, 38: 132–134.

McTaggart, J. M. E. (1927) *The Nature of Existence*, Vol. 2. Cambridge: Cambridge University Press.

Menzel, Christopher (1990) "Actualism, Ontological Commitment, and Possible Worlds Semantics," *Synthese* 85: 355–389.

(1991) "The True Modal Logic," *Journal of Philosophical Logic* 20: 331–374.

Morris, Thomas (1987) "Properties, Modalities, and God," in his *Anselmian Explorations*. Notre Dame, IN: University of Notre Dame Press.

Mumford, Stephen (2003) *Dispositions*. Oxford: Oxford University Press.

Munitz, M. K. (1951) "One Universe or Many?" *Journal of the History of Ideas* 12: 231–255.

O'Connor, Timothy (2012) *Theism and Ultimate Explanation: The Necessary Shape of Contingency*. Oxford: Wiley-Blackwell.

Oppy, Graham (2006) *Arguing about Gods*. Cambridge: Cambridge University Press.

(2014) *Describing Gods*. Cambridge: Cambridge University Press.

Newlands, Samuel (2013) "Spinoza's Modal Metaphysics," *The Stanford Encyclopedia of Philosophy*, Edward N. Zalta (ed.), https://plato.stanford.edu/archives/win2013/entries/spinoza-modal/.

Philoponus, John (1987) *Against Aristotle, on the Eternity of the World*. London: Duckworth.

Philoponus, John and Simplicius (1987) *Place, Void, and Eternity*. Ithaca NY: Cornell University Press.

Plantinga, Alvin (1967) *God and Other Minds*. Ithaca, NY: Cornell University Press.

(1974a) *God, Freedom, and Evil*. New York, NY: Harper and Row.

(1974b) *The Nature of Necessity*. Oxford: Oxford University Press.

(1976) "Actualism and Possible Worlds," *Theoria* 42: 139–160.

Prior, Arthur (1956) "Modality and Quantification in S5," *Journal of Symbolic Logic* 21: 60–62.

(1957) *Time and Modality*. Oxford: Clarendon Press.

(1962) "Limited Indeterminism," *Review of Metaphysics* 16 (1): 55–61.

(1977) *Worlds, Times, and Selves*. Amherst, MA: University of Massachusetts Press.

Pruss, Alexander (2006) *The Principle of Sufficient Reason*. Cambridge: Cambridge University Press.

(2009a) "From Grim Reaper to the Kalaam," http://alexanderpruss .blogspot.com/2009/10/from-grim-reaper-paradox-to-kalaam.html.

(2009b) "Leibnizian Cosmological Arguments," in W. L. Craig and J. P. Moreland (eds.), *Blackwell Companion to Natural Theology*. Oxford: Blackwell. 24–100.

Rasmussen, Josh (2012) "Presentists May Say Goodbye to A-Properties," *Analysis* 72: 270–276.

Reichenbach, Bruce, (2017) "Cosmological Argument," *The Stanford Encyclopedia of Philosophy* (Winter Edition), Edward N. Zalta (ed.), https://plato.stanford.edu/archives/win2017/entries/cosmological-argument.

Rescher, Nicholas (2013) *On Leibniz*. Pittsburgh, PA: University of Pittsburgh Press.

Ross, James (1969) *Philosophical Theology*. Indianapolis, IN: Bobbs-Merrill.

Rowe, William L. (1988) *The Cosmological Argument*. Bronx, NY: Fordham University Press.

(2007) *Philosophy of Religion: An Introduction*, 4th edn. Belmont, CA: Wadsworth.

(2015) "An Examination of the Cosmological Argument," in Michael Rea and Louis Pojman (eds.), *Philosophy of Religion : An Anthology*, 7th edn. Stamford, CT: Cengage Learning. 167–176.

Russell, Bertrand (1905) "On Denoting," *Mind* 14: 479–493.

Salmon, Nathan (1987) "Existence," in J. Tomberlin (ed.), *Philosophical Perspectives*, vol. 1. Atascadero, CA: Ridgeview Press. 49–108.

Schnieder, Benjamin and Steinberg, Alex (2016) "Without Reason?" *Pacific Philosophical Quarterly* 97: 523–541.

Sider, Ted (1997) "Four Dimensionalism," *Philosophical Review* 106: 197–231.

(2001) *Four Dimensionalism: An Ontology of Persistence and Time.* Oxford: Oxford University Press.

Skow, Bradford (2015) *Objective Becoming.* Oxford: Oxford University Press.

Skyrms, Bryan (1976) "Possible Worlds, Physics and Metaphysics," *Philosophical Studies* 30 (5): 323–332.

Smith, Quentin (1995) "A Defense of a Principle of Sufficient Reason," *Metaphilosophy* 26 (½): 97–106.

(2008) "A Cosmological Argument for a Self-Caused Universe" https://infidels.org/library/modern/quentin_smith/self-caused.html.

Sorensen, Roy (2003) *A Brief History of the Paradox.* Oxford: Oxford University Press.

Spinoza, Benedict de (1949) *Ethics,* James Gutmann (ed.). New York, NY: Hafner Press.

Stalnaker, Robert (1976) "Possible Worlds," *Noûs* 10 (1): 65–75.

Stump, Eleonore (2003) *Aquinas.* London: Routledge.

Swinburne, Richard (1993) *The Coherence of Theism,* revised edn. Oxford: Oxford University Press.

(2004) *The Existence of God,* 2nd edn. Oxford: Oxford University Press.

Thomson, J. F. (1954) "Tasks and Super-Tasks," *Analysis* 15 (1): 1–13.

Turner, Donald (2003) "The Many-Universes Solution to the Problem of Evil," in Richard Gale and Alexander Pruss (eds.), *The Existence of God.* United Kingdom: Ashgate Publishers.

(2014) "Revisiting the Many-Universes Solution to the Problem of Evil," in Klaas Kraay (ed.), *God and the Multiverse.* New York, NY: Routledge.

Vallicella, William F. (1997) "On an Insufficient Argument against Sufficient Reason," *Ratio* 10 (1): 76–81.

van Inwagen, Peter (1983) *An Essay on Free Will.* Oxford: Clarendon Press.

(1986), "Two Concepts of Possible Worlds," *Midwest Studies in Philosophy, XI,* P. French, T. Uehling, and H. Wettstein (eds.) Minneapolis, MN: University of Minnesota Press. 185–213.

(2009) *Metaphysics,* 3rd edn. Boulder, CO: Westview Press.

Williams, Robert (2008) "Chances, Counterfactuals, and Similarity," *Philosophy and Phenomenological Research* 77: 385–420.

Williamson, Timothy (2002) "Necessary Existents," in A. O'Hear (ed.), *Royal Institute of Philosophy Supplement*. Cambridge: Cambridge University Press. 269–287.

(2013) *Modal Logic as Metaphysics*. Oxford: Oxford University Press.

Wolfson, H. A. (1966) "Patristic Arguments against the Eternity of the World," *Harvard Theological Review* 59: 354–367.

(1976) *The Philosophy of the Kalam*. Cambridge, MA: Harvard University Press.

Made in the USA
Coppell, TX
23 January 2020